This little church
had none

Everyone in church leadership should read this book — and then encourage their followers to do the same!
(John Blanchard, Christian author, international conference speaker and evangelist)

This Little Church Had None should be read by anyone who cares to know why the church at large is in an unhealthy state and what is the prescription for its resuscitation.
(Christopher Cone, President, Tyndale Theological Seminary & Biblical Institute)

This Little Church Had None ... is a desperately needed message for these uncertain times, written with clarity, spiritual wisdom, biblical precision and a passion that reflects the authors' own deep love for the truth
(John MacArthur, Grace Community Church, Sun Valley, CA)

Sales of this book help to promote the missionary work of EP in making good Christian literature available at affordable prices in poorer countries of the world and training pastors and preachers to teach God's Word to others.

This little church
had none

A CHURCH IN SEARCH
OF THE TRUTH

**Dr Gary E. Gilley
with Jay Wegter**

 BOOKS

EP Books
Faverdale North, Darlington, DL3 0PH, England

e-mail: sales@epbooks.org

EP Books US
P. O. Box 614, Carlisle, PA 17013, USA

e-mail: usasales@epbooks.org

web: http://www.epbooks.org

First published 2009

British Library Cataloguing in Publication Data available

ISBN-13 978 085234 708 9   ISBN 0 85234 708 1

Unless otherwise indicated Scripture quotations are taken from the NEW AMERICAN STANDARD BIBLE®, Copyright © 1960, 1962, 1963, 1968, 1971, 1972, 1973, 1975, 1977, 1995 by the Lockman Foundation. Used by permission.

Printed in the United States of America

This book is dedicated to
Esther Rader,
who faithfully served our Lord
as church secretary for almost three decades.
(Gary Gilley)

and

To my wife,
Michele,
who excels in showing grace
(Jay Wegter)

Contents

Preface

A few years ago I wrote a book entitled *This Little Church Went to Market — The church in the age of entertainment.* There I explored in detail areas in which I believe the 'seeker-sensitive' church model is missing the mark biblically, especially in regard to its gospel and doctrinal messages. That book was followed by *This Little Church Stayed Home — A faithful church in deceptive times.* The original intent was to identify the marks of a truly biblical church standing firm in the face of wide-scale assaults by the forces of deception. While a portion of that volume was in fact dedicated to this objective, I also felt compelled specifically to address the areas of deception surrounding the rapidly growing emergent church movement. In this, the third book in the 'Little Church' series, I want to talk about 'a church in search of truth'. My contention is that the great need of the moment is for Christ's church to rediscover the truth that it has either lost or minimized, to understand the inestimable value of the truth in the lives of God's people and to recognize its role as the supporter and dispenser of that truth (1 Tim. 3:15).

I have entitled this book *This Little Church Had None — A church in search of truth* because I believe that the majority of so-called evangelical churches and Christians have lost, or at least misplaced, this important mandate. Truth has been sacrificed on the altars of pragmatism, church growth, postmodern ideologies, paganism and hedonism, to name a few. In many cases this defection from truth is not so much by design as the result of ignorance and neglect. A whole generation of believers has grown up in churches in which the Word of God has not been systematically taught and appreciated. While there are notable and happy exceptions to this, nevertheless we should not be surprised to find that the people of this generation have marginalized the place of the Scriptures in their lives.

I recently ministered at a church in which the leaders knew that they had drifted from their biblical roots and wanted to re-establish their ministry around God's Word. In my discussion with the leadership one man mentioned that it had been twenty years since they had had a pastor who had taught them the great doctrines of the faith and systematically expounded the Scriptures. How can we expect such Christians, Christians who have lived their lives largely outside the parameters of God's truth, to appreciate and desire the centrality of the Word in their lives? After all, these very people have built large churches, funded major ministries, travelled worldwide on mission trips, shown compassion to the poor and needy, and much more, all without the benefit of biblically based lives and churches.

Exactly why should the Bible be returned to centre stage? Evangelicalism has never appeared healthier, in the USA at least. Megachurches dot our landscape; money is abundant (at least for the more popular ministries); evangelical superstars write books that are read by millions and appear on television talk shows regularly; the evangelical right can make or break a politician, Rick Warren's P.E.A.C.E. plan is organizing the global church to win the war on poverty, sickness and illiteracy, etc. What more could we want? Christians are now respected in the marketplace of ideas; we have an impact on culture and influence the political agenda. How could anyone not recognize the great progress made by the followers of Christ over the last thirty years?

Yet something is missing. Pollsters have confirmed that this modern brand of evangelicalism is not changing lives — evangelicals live in much the same way as their unsaved counterparts. Church attendance has grown in the megachurches, but not overall. As a percentage, taken as a whole, church growth has remained stagnant for years, and millions of people have dropped out of the church. Christians are biblically illiterate and spurn doctrinal issues. The Bible remains the best-selling book in the world, but few read it and fewer still turn to Scripture for their understanding of life, or even of God. It is as though the heart has been extracted from the patient, but few have noticed because the sick person is being kept alive through artificial means.

Among the artificial solutions being offered for our spiritual problems there is an almost frantic search by many for an alternative form of Christianity that would seem more authentic to them. Studies by George Barna have revealed a number of such alternatives, some more biblically sound than others. He writes:

Each of six alternatives was deemed by most adults to be 'a complete and biblically valid way for someone who does NOT participate in the services or activities of a conventional church to experience and express their faith in God'. Those alternatives include engaging in faith activities at home, with one's family (considered acceptable by 89% of adults); being active in a house church (75%); watching a religious television program (69%); listening to a religious radio broadcast (68%); attending a special ministry event, such as a concert or community service activity (68%); and participating in a marketplace ministry (54%). Smaller proportions of the public consider other alternatives to be complete and biblically valid ways of experiencing and expressing their faith in God. Those include interacting with a faith-oriented website (45%) and participating in live events via the Internet (42%).[1]

It is my contention that what is needed is not alternative forms so much as a return to truth as revealed through the Word. The writer of Hebrews tells us that God 'spoke long ago to the fathers in the prophets in many portions and in many ways' (Heb. 1:1), and in that form revealed the truths found in the Old Testament.

The Old Testament revelation was supplemented by the New Testament because God 'in these last days has spoken to us in His Son' (Heb. 1:2). This communication of God through his Son was passed on through the apostles: 'After it was at the first spoken through the Lord, it was confirmed to us by those who heard' (Heb. 2:3). We therefore possess through the Scriptures the complete revelation of God for these 'last days', a revelation that is 'inspired by God and profitable for teaching, for reproof, for correction, for training in righteousness; so that the man of God may be adequate, equipped for every good work' (2 Tim. 3:16-17).

This beloved passage from 2 Timothy is quoted by all segments of the Christian faith, but is apparently not believed by many. We rejoice in the fact that God has 'breathed out' his Word so that we can hold in our hands and read with our eyes the inspired communication of God. But we baulk at the idea that God's Word is 'adequate [to] equip [us] for *every good work*' (emphasis mine). Or as Peter says, 'His divine power has granted to us *everything pertaining to life and godliness*, through the true knowledge of Him who called us by His own glory and excellence' (2 Peter 1:3, emphasis mine). It is the emphasized words in these texts that many refuse to believe. We are most happy to possess the inspired Word of God as long as it does not interfere with our own preconceived notions and learned ideas about how life 'really works'. We are thrilled by the Bible stories and are most grateful that the Scriptures reveal the path to God and eternal life, but real-life issues must be addressed by other sources. The Word is apparently mute when it comes to emotional problems, marital struggles, personal and interpersonal conflicts and a host of other predicaments. For these types of concerns we turn to human wisdom in its various forms. As a result our churches too often pay lip service to God's Word but look to man's word for true solutions and direction. If this is our mind-set it should not surprise us that the Bible, while venerated, is seldom consulted on the pertinent matters of life. A few years of such neglect, and the Word becomes a much-loved museum piece, not a life-changing force looked to first and last for God's instruction and direction. The Lord may claim that his Word is sharper than any two-edged sword (Heb. 4:12), but, kept in its sheath, its power appears rather dull to the average believer.

Take church management and organization, for example. The structure of the local church is now informed more by business techniques (Rick Warren's mentor is business management guru Peter Drucker), surveys (George Barna is referred to more often than the apostle Paul) and pragmatism ('what works') than by anything the Scriptures might have to say on the subject. Observing today's church one might get the idea that the Bible had nothing at all to say about how a church is to function. A new convert, reading the New Testament for the first time, might be totally puzzled to find the book of Acts, the Pastoral Epistles (1 and 2 Timothy and Titus) and inspired letters such as Colossians and Ephesians which lay out so clearly God's paradigm for his church. Such a novice might correctly ask the modern church why it is consulting so many experts but not the divine manual on church life.

The same uninitiated new believer might be equally surprised at first by sermons that only superficially draw from the Scriptures; 'Christian counselling' that is rooted in Freud or Rogers with an occasional Bible verse thrown into the mix; Christian youth ministries that attract by means of fun, music and/or mysticism, but provide virtually no training in God's truth; and support groups that are modelled after Alcoholics Anonymous rather than the New Testament. Given time, our new disciple catches on — the church is really not that much different from the other clubs, self-help groups and social organizations that were part of his or her unconverted life. To be sure, in many evangelical circles you hear a little more about Jesus; an occasional prayer is offered; a few choruses are sung, and popular verses of Scripture and slogans thrown around — but little more. The average Christian is marching to the same beat as his unbelieving counterpart, both living out their own patchwork philosophies of life based upon a mix of pragmatism, social standards and faddish ideologies, with a dash of Scripture added (if you doubt this make sure you read the introduction and chapter 7).

Sadly, this is how many children of God have been raised by their leaders. They have no idea that Christ has called them to something more — lives truly based upon the truth of his Word. And if they have a vague suspicion that there is something more, something deeper, something better, than the life they are experiencing, they have no concept where to search for it. These deficiencies are increasingly being recognized by the mainstream evangelical church, but the remedy is not (see chapter 1). What is needed is a return to full confidence in the power and the authority of the Word of God, which in turn will cause church leaders to teach once again the full counsel of the Lord. But there are many obstacles in the way of such a return to the centrality of the Word. We will discuss these obstacles in Part I, then suggest a pathway back to a church firmly founded on truth in Part II. The final part will address the issue of evangelism in a postmodern world.

Gary E. Gilley

Introduction

Ever since my college days I have enjoyed the study of philosophy. It is fascinating to delve into the reasoning of thinkers like Plato, Descartes or Kant and study how they pieced life together. However, I have always deliberated on these philosophies from a biblical vantage point. That is, I have found their ideas interesting, yet largely flawed in the light of the teachings of Scripture. But, as I examined the writings of such philosophers, I have often thought about the reaction of unbelievers to the same concepts. For one thing is very noticeable about philosophies — they are constantly changing. As each new philosopher comes along, he rejects the views of the previous one. Each generation considers the last generation, with its set of ideas, systems of thought and social structures, as passé, apparently not recognizing that the next generation will cast the same censorious comments on the current one.

This constant flux concerning truth must be most frustrating to those without Christ as they observe historically the changing views of thinking people. Even within our own lifetimes the rapid presentation of new worldviews that promised to solve the 'mysteries of life' — only to be soon relegated to the philosophical rubbish heap and replaced with the newest idea on the block — has to be unsettling. It is no wonder that postmodernism has taken root in Western thinking. After all, if Plato, Descartes, Kant and a whole train-load of others have presented unique systems of truth, only to be rejected and contradicted by the next set of thinkers, after a while one begins to assume that maybe there is no such thing as objective, universal truth. Perhaps what remains is selective truth, temporary truth, individual truth (truth for you, but not for me). If the 'truth claims' of the best and brightest from the past have not proved true, then what hope do we have that the next philosophy will offer the key to life's issues? In a real sense, after thousands of years riding the merry-go-round of philosophical thought, people have grown tired and want to get off the ride. There apparently is no absolute truth. There is no final authority. There is no one whose ideas are superior to anyone else's. We are left with relativism — let each of us do his own thing and believe his own way and let's just accept one another's ideas as equal. Eventually all of this rings hollow. Postmodernism, which challenges absolute truth and embraces relativism, has been birthed from the ashes of disillusionment.

Popular film star Brad Pitt, in an interview with *Rolling Stone* magazine, expressed well the disillusionment that many face today. Pitt was discussing a character (Tyler) whom he played in the movie *Fight Club*:

> **Pitt:** The point is, the question has to be asked: 'What track are we on?' Tyler starts out in the movie saying, 'Man, I know all these things are supposed to seem important to us — the car, the condo, our versions of success — but if that's the case, why is the general feeling out there reflecting more impotence and isolation and desperation and loneliness?' If you ask me, I say, 'Toss all this, we gotta find something else.' Because all I know is that at this point in time, we are heading for a dead end, a numbing of the soul, a complete atrophy of the spiritual being. And I don't want that.

> **RS:** So if we're heading toward this kind of existential dead end in society, what do you think should happen?

Pitt: Hey, man, I don't have those answers yet. The emphasis now is on success and personal gain. [Smiles] I'm
sitting in it, and I'm telling you, that's not it.

RS: But, and I'm glad you said it first, people will read your
saying that and think...

Pitt: I'm the guy who's got everything. I know. But I'm telling
you, once you get everything, then you're just left with
yourself. I've said it before and I'll say it again: It doesn't
help you sleep any better, and you don't wake up any
better because of it. Now, no one's going to want to
hear that. I understand it. I'm sorry I'm the guy who's
got to say it. But I'm telling you.[1]

Of course postmodernism did not invent disillusionment; it is
the ultimate trademark of any philosophical or religious system
that denies the truth of the biblical understanding of the reality of
life. In T. S. Eliot's poem 'The Hollow Men' we find the same
struggle:

This is the way the way the world ends,
This is the way the way the world ends,
This is the way the way the world ends,
Not with a bang but a whimper.

There is something within the nature of man that rejects this
type of existence and end. There has to be more to our life than
what many experience. Something has gone wrong but, having
already factored out the biblical view of reality, people are forced
to turn to false sources for a handle on life. Having missed the
fountain of life, they must dig other wells (Jer. 2:13).

The Scripture has a different story to tell. Paul informs us in
Romans 1:19-23 that man's problem is that he has suppressed the
truth about God which has been revealed in the creation around
him. This suppression has led to darkened hearts and imaginations
that are empty of spiritual reality. Man tries to fill in the blanks with

whatever might be in vogue at the moment — in biblical times it was idols and the direct, conscious worship of creation. Today it might be New Age philosophy, Eastern religions, human achievement, humanistic theory, modernistic certainty, postmodern uncertainty, or any number of other ideas. The bottom line is that mankind has rejected God and his truth and suffers the consequences of that choice as God hands him over to enslavement by his own worldview, with its resulting sins (Rom. 1:24-32). It is no wonder people are disillusioned with life; sin and false beliefs ultimately have that effect. As the world system propagates its various views and philosophies we should expect nothing less than minds scratching about in empty speculation and foolish hearts wandering around in darkness (Rom. 1:21).

The pillar of truth

Enter the church. One of the things that separate the church from all other organizations is that it is to be the pillar and support of the truth (1 Tim. 3:15). The congregation which is not functioning as the support and dispenser of truth falls short of the biblical criteria for a local church; therefore the assembly which does not major on truth does not fit the definition of a New Testament church. Its attendance may be 'mega', its programs prolific, its enthusiasm contagious and its motives honourable, but if it is not the pillar and support of truth it fails in its job description as a church. Call it a club, a social gathering, a political-awareness group, a socially concerned assembly, or an entertainment centre, but don't call it a church.

The church that has God's understanding of truth will begin thinking biblically. This is often called 'a biblical worldview'. In attempting to discern how widespread a biblical worldview is today (or how similar the beliefs of people are to the teaching of Scripture) pollster George Barna developed a rather minimalist list of required beliefs. They were as follows:

1. Believing that absolute moral truth exists.
2. Believing that such truth is defined by the Bible.
3. And the firm belief in six specific religious views:
   - Jesus Christ lived a sinless life.
   - God is the all-powerful and all-knowing Creator of the universe and He still rules today.
   - Salvation is a gift from God and cannot be earned.
   - Satan is a living force.
   - A Christian has a responsibility to share their faith in Christ with other people.
   - The Bible is accurate in all its teachings.[2]

As stated above, this is a barebones list. With the addition of even a few other essentials of the Christian faith (e.g. the bodily resurrection of Jesus, the bodily resurrection of people, the actual existence of heaven and hell, eternal judgment, the virgin birth, the Scriptures as the inspired Word of God, etc.), the numbers heralded as having a biblical worldview would plummet drastically. As it is, the statistics are startling. In 2007 Barna identified 40% of Americans as born again (this statistic is highly suspect to me, but we will go with it for now) and 7% as evangelical Christians. The results of the study indicated that 'most Americans do not have strong and clear beliefs, largely because they do not possess a coherent biblical worldview... Most Americans have one foot in the biblical camp, and one foot outside it.'[3]

In Barna's most recent study it was discovered that only 9% of those who he claims are born again have a biblical worldview.[4] In a later survey of the clergy it was found that only 51% of Protestant pastors have a biblical worldview, even by Barna's minimalist definition. He states, 'The low percentage of Christians who have a biblical worldview is a direct reflection of the fact that half of our primary religious teachers and leaders do not have one.'[5] But it gets worse:

The research also points out that even in churches where the pastor has a biblical worldview, most of the congregants do not. More than six out of every seven congregants in the typical church do not share the biblical worldview of their pastor even when he or she has one.[6]

To develop a biblical worldview in a congregation requires:

> ... a lot of purposeful activity: teaching, prayer, conversation, accountability, and so forth. [However] if the 51% of pastors who have a biblical worldview were to strategically and relentlessly assist their congregants in adopting such a way of interpreting and responding to life, the impact on our churches, families and society at-large would be enormous.[7]

To this end this book is dedicated. We shall seek to understand the opposition to having and living a biblical worldview, identify what steps we must take to implement the same in our churches, and then consider how to evangelize people from the framework of a biblical worldview.

PART I

OBSTACLES TO TRUTH

1

The Seeker-Sensitive Adjustment

The church attempting to draw its cues from the Scriptures rather than the culture is always facing obstacles from one source or another. One of the most challenging obstacles for this last generation of believers has come from those attempting, most often in good faith, to broaden the outreach of the local church. While some helpful methods, programs and concepts have resulted from this attempt, sadly some serious compromise has been introduced as well.

I have detailed the issues that I have with the watered-down gospel message and doctrinal weakness of what I have termed the 'new-paradigm church' (or, better, the 'market-driven' or 'seeker-sensitive' model) in my earlier book, *This Little Church Went to Market*. Therefore, I will not go over that ground again here, except to say that the predictable outcome of ignoring the biblical approach to 'doing church', as some call it, has borne fruit, and it is not pretty. Careful observers from within the seeker-sensitive movement, as well as from detractors, have recognized that this model has not produced what it has promised. Rather, a weakened form of the church has come to life — a church brimming with activity, flush with money and offering the finest in everything, but failing to produce much in the way of disciples.

This is not to say that no one in a new-paradigm church is a true disciple of Christ. That is simply not the case. But, for all the bluster and commotion, very little is actually happening, especially if you define disciples as those whose lives have been changed by Christ. Virtually every survey taken in recent decades has confirmed that so-called evangelicals are living no differently from the unsaved when it comes to morals, ethics and values. Of late, even leaders within the market-driven church have recognized that there is something seriously wrong with their model. George Barna, for example, virtually the architect of the new-paradigm church, has now distanced himself from it and headed in the direction of the emergent church (see my book *This Little Church Stayed Home* for more on the emerging/emergent church). The discerning Christian might be careful about following Barna in his new emerging endeavour, given his failed effort in reconstruction of the church in the past. Nevertheless, fresh evidence is available that all is not well with the seeker-sensitive movement, and that evidence comes from a reliable source.

Willow Creek

Recently things have been a bit tough for the Willow Creek Community Church, the flagship congregation of the 'seeker-sensitive' movement. It is a well-known fact that Willow Creek has set the pace for thirty years in its redesign of the local church. More recently Rick Warren and his Saddleback Community Church have stolen the spotlight from Willow Creek and, to some degree, eclipsed its influence on new-paradigm churches. But, rest assured, Willow Creek, along with its Willow Creek Association, which boasts 12,000 member churches from ninety denominations, is still charting the way for those who look to 'felt needs', surveys, the latest innovations and market strategy, instead of Scripture, for their structuring of the local church.[1] When Willow Creek speaks, church leaders listen. When Willow marches out a new product or method, churches around the globe fall in line. Whatever Willow promotes, others emulate.

So, as I said, it has been tough going during the last few years for Willow Creek and for its followers as well. It was only in September 2006 that Willow put up the shutters on its highly acclaimed Axis experiment. Axis was Willow's 'church-within-a-church' designed for people in their twenties. At one point the ten-year project boasted 2,000 worshippers at services designed especially for Generation Xers,[2] but numbers had fallen to 350 when the leadership decided to shut it down. What Willow discovered was that:

> Axis didn't connect young adults with the rest of the congregation. Once they outgrew the service, Axis members found it hard to transition into the rest of the Chicago-area megachurch. Young adults also struggled to meet and develop relationships with mentors in the larger congregation.[3]

Who would have thought that separating the young adults from the body of Christ for a decade would result in integration issues when they grew older? Somebody must have missed the fine print in a Barna survey! At any rate, Willow recognized its error and incorporated Axis into the larger congregation. This move came too late, however, for hundreds of Willow clones who were locked into step with the mother church. Many started similar church-within-a-church congregations under Willow's leadership and most of these groups will now suffer the same fate.

As humiliating as the Axis failure must have been for Willow Creek, the latest bombshell dwarfs it by comparison. Willow's leadership now admits, in the words of Bill Hybels, 'We made a mistake.' Hybels, founder and senior pastor of Willow Creek Community Church and chairman of the board of the Willow Creek Association, is referring to Willow Creek's philosophical and ministerial approach to 'doing' church. This is the approach pioneered by Hybels and company, honed to perfection and disseminated to eager church leaders worldwide. This is the approach which distinguishes the seeker-sensitive model from other models. It is this approach that Hybels now admits was a mistake.

Willow Creek's confession

First, let me say that I admire Willow's transparency and humility on this matter. Not many people or groups would make a public admission of error of this magnitude. Actually to admit that the model of 'doing church' into which they have poured thirty years and millions of dollars has been a mistake is incredible. This is not to say that Willow's confession is without flaw, for while they profess mistakes they still apparently think they have done pretty well. And they still believe that they are the ones to lead the church into the future, even if they have been wrong for three decades. But more on that later; for now, what are the specifics of the confession?

One of the executive pastors of Willow Creek, Greg Hawkins, became deeply concerned that, despite all the efforts of the megachurch, perhaps they were not being as effective as they thought. As he watched people dropping money into the offering plate week after week, the thought nagged him: 'Are we spending those folk's money in the right way?'[4] In 2004, with Hybels' permission, Hawkins led a study of the congregation asking the people how effective the programs and ministry of Willow Creek had been in their lives. Later Hawkins turned to thirty other Willow Creek Association churches to see if the results of the study at Willow would be comparable at these churches — they were. These results, which have been published in a new book, *Reveal: Where Are You?*, have been described by Hybels as everything from 'earth-breaking' to 'mind-blowing' in a disturbing way.

What are the specifics? Hawkins defines Willow's ministerial goal as 'trying to help people who are far from Christ become disciples of Christ characterized by their love for God and other people'. This is a most commendable goal, but how has Willow gone about trying to accomplish it? Hawkins states:

We do that by creating a variety of programs and services for people to participate in. Our strategy is to try to get people, far from Christ, engaged in these activities. The more people are participating in these sets of activities with higher levels of frequency it will produce disciples of Christ.

This has been Willow's methodology of discipleship throughout the years — the philosophy that has been transported and reproduced around the globe. But what was revealed, via the multi-year, multi-church study, was disturbing. Hawkins identifies three major discoveries.

The first is that increasing levels of participation in these activities do not predict whether a person will become a disciple of Christ.

Secondly, in every church there is a spiritual continuum in which 'you can look at your congregation and put them [the people] in one of five unique segments. The segments are aligned around people's intimacy with Jesus Christ and how important that relationship with Christ is to their lives.' The segments into which a local church's people can be neatly slipped are:

Segment 1 — Those who are just exploring Christianity. Therefore, these are non-believers who are attending services or activities provided by the church (i.e. unbelievers).

Segment 2 — Those who love Jesus and have a relationship with him and are growing in that relationship but are fairly new in that relationship (i.e. new Christians).

Segment 3 — Those who are close to Christ; their relationship with Christ is important to them on a daily basis. These are people who 'might pray, read the Bible and have thoughts of God' on a daily basis (i.e. given the parameters of this study, these would be nominal believers, who have a definite interest in Christ but are not 'fully devoted followers' of the Lord).

Segment 4 — Those who centre their lives on their relationship with Christ. Their relationship with Christ is the most important relationship in their entire lives (Hybels calls these 'fully devoted followers of Christ').

Segment 5 — Believers who are stalled in their relationship with Christ. They are not investing time on a regular basis in their relationship with Christ. Although they are actually investing time in church events on a regular basis, they are not investing time in their personal relationship with Christ (i.e. nominal Christians).

The third 'ground-breaking' discovery was that each of the segments had different needs, yet most churches deal with them as if 'one size fits all'. Also, the church activities that most churches provide are most helpful in the first two segments. 'Churches do great things to help people in those segments,' Hybels states. But the activities that seem to be helpful to the first two groups are less helpful for the last three segments. As a result, the study showed that 'It is the ones in the first two segments who are the most satisfied with local churches.' For instance, people who are not yet Christians gave Willow Creek top marks, and new believers were not far behind. However, 'The last three segments have increasing dissatisfaction; they are disappointed with the role that the local church is playing in their lives.' The third segment, described by Hybels as growing Christians, were much less pleased, and the 'fully devoted followers of Christ' (segment 4) were quite unhappy with Willow. This group says that 'They are not being fed; they want more of the meat of the Word of God; serious-minded Scripture taught to them; they want to be challenged more.' And increasingly those in segment four (the 'fully devoted to Christ' segment), are thinking about leaving the local church. Which is, Hawkins laments, 'incredibly sad; the people who love God the most are the most disappointed by their local church'!

In response Hawkins told Hybels:

We've made a mistake. What we should have done [as people became Christians, was that] we should have started telling people and teaching people that they have to take responsibility to become self-feeders. We should have gotten people, taught them how to read their Bibles between services, do the spiritual practices much more aggressively on their own because what's happening to these people, the older they get the more they are expecting the church to feed them, when in fact the more mature a Christian becomes the more he becomes a self-feeder.

In order to remedy these 'mind-blowing' mistakes, the leadership at Willow is working hard 'to rethink how we coach people to full spiritual development'. They are pioneering 'personal spiritual growth plans — customized spiritual growth plans for everyone at Willow'.

Hawkins admits, 'All of what we are discovering is rocking our world at our church.' And it should be, for Hybels owns up:

Some of the stuff that we have put millions of dollars into, thinking it would really help our people grow and develop spiritually, when the data came back it wasn't helping people that much. Other things that we didn't put that much money into and didn't put much staff against is stuff our people are crying out for.[5]

In the light of this study Hybels tells us, 'I got the wake-up call of my adult life... [It was] one of the hardest things I have ever had to digest as a leader.'

What Hawkins and Hybels have discovered are things that many churches have always known, although they have often been intimidated by the megachurches into believing they were wrong. They are discovering:

- That financial prosperity and high attendance figures do not tell us whether we have a church that pleases God. The Lord never provided statistics concerning the church membership or attendance of the local churches in the New Testament. And the two churches (out of seven) given great marks in Revelation chapters 2 and 3 were apparently small and poor (Rev. 2:8-11; 3:7-13), while the churches who seemed to have got their act together were rebuked severely by the Lord (Rev. 3:1-6,14-22).

• That participation in programs does not produce authentic disciples of Christ. While every church has programs, the Scriptures teach that it is the Word of God through the power of the Spirit that changes lives.

• That unbelievers and baby Christians will attend a good show, and even give high marks for the production, but those who hunger for true spiritual life will be not be content with such entertainment.

• That whatever is used to draw people to the church must be continued if you want to keep them. If you attract people through entertainment and superficial teaching, most will not hang around if you shift to solid exposition of the Word and God-honouring ministries.

• That attempting to reach people for Christ through meeting their felt needs is a bottomless pit. Christ-centred people are not likely to be developed by creating programs that cater to their self-centredness.

• That churches based on the foundation of secular research, group opinion or surveys may produce a congregation that pleases people for a time, but these things will not produce a church that pleases God. God has already given his design for the church in the New Testament; it is neither necessary nor right for us to ignore that design and create our own.

Implications

What does all of this mean to us? What are we to do now? Hawkins offers two implications:

First, we need to ask different questions. We need to go beyond asking how many [people are coming to our services and events]. We need to ask, are the things we are doing helping people grow in their intimacy with Christ? We need to ask not just leaders, but participants, what they need, what's working and what is not working.

Secondly, Hawkins says, 'We cannot do this alone.' Willow therefore invites us to tell them what is working and not working in our churches. In order to expedite this sharing of pragmatic ideas Willow has entered into a whole new round of research. They have invited 500 additional churches (they must be members of the Willow Creek Association) to participate in a survey that will give them more data.

Where will all of this lead? It is important to ponder Hawkins' idea carefully at this point. He states:

> Here is our dream — that we fundamentally change the way we do church; that we *take out a clean sheet of paper, and rethink all of our old assumptions*, replace them with new insights, insights that are informed by research and rooted in Scripture. Our dream is to discover what God is doing and how He is asking us to *join Him in transforming this planet* (emphasis mine).

An analysis

There are three issues, summarized well in the above statement, that are very disturbing.

First, *haven't we heard all of this before?* Isn't this exactly what Hybels and the architects of the seeker-sensitive movement told us thirty years ago? Whether or not they used those exact words, the central theme of the movement was that we must 'change the way we do church. We must take out a clean sheet of paper, and rethink all of our old assumptions and replace them with new insights.' For three decades now the evangelical church, to a large degree, has been operating on the basis of the insights developed by Willow Creek. As they look back, Willow has recognized that the programs they developed on the basis of these insights were faulty — they did not accomplish their stated purpose; they have led the church as a whole down a futile pathway for a generation.

Even the 'fully devoted followers of Christ' (the fourth segment of the congregation) give us pause. This is the group, within Willow Creek circles, that is the most spiritually mature, yet even they don't know how to read their Bibles or feed themselves. Willow's strategy for the future is not to adjust their services and ministries to feed this spiritually hungry group; their plan is to teach them how to feed themselves. And while I will admit that it is important to teach people how to feed themselves, I have to ask, 'Why should these serious-minded believers bother to come to Willow-type services at all? Why not find good churches that are taking care of the flock in a biblical manner?' After all, Ephesians 4:11-16 is clear that it is the responsibility of the church leadership to equip the saints through the teaching of the Word of God.

Having failed at virtually every level to produce true disciples and develop biblical churches, now Willow want to start all over again, and they would like to take us with them. We can trust them this time, we are assured, for they have new research tools, new insights and new programs. They will guide us correctly this time — that is a promise. This is a bit hard to believe, but Hybels and Hawkins are so winsome in their presentations, so sincere in their promises, that millions will undoubtedly follow them once again, blindly, with Bibles firmly left unexamined, down the road on this new adventure.

My second concern is that *we are being called to join God in 'transforming this planet'*. Since when has it been God's design to use the church to transform the planet? I know this is the common rhetoric heard throughout evangelicalism recently, but it does not find its basis in Scripture. There is no question that believers must take seriously their role as citizens of this earth. We should protect its resources, be involved with helping the poor and needy and reach out to the marginalized with the love of Christ. But primarily we are called to join God, as it were, to make disciples (Matt. 28:19,20) and to herald the gospel which is able to rescue people 'from the domain of darkness', and transfer them 'to the kingdom of His beloved Son' (Col. 1:13); we are not called to help God transform the planet. He will do that in his own timing, and without our help, when Christ comes again (2 Peter 3:10-13).

However, the most disturbing element in this statement is that *once again Scripture takes a back seat to pragmatism*. Research and methods are the key to 'new insights' and the next direction for the church, not the Word of God. In Hawkins' and Hybels' two videos, only once is Scripture mentioned, when Hawkins talks about new insights 'that are informed by research and rooted in Scripture'. While the New Testament contains God's instructions for his church, no actual text of Scripture is mentioned by either man. Instead Hawkins is lining up 500 Willow Creek Association churches to ask them, 'What is working for you?' The Willow system was originally steeped in pragmatism rather than Scripture, and it appears that nothing has changed. They are once again going to the well of pragmatism — tell them 'what works', and they will develop programs and methods which will accomplish their goals. Pragmatism has always been at the heart of the seeker-sensitive movement, and it still is. Willow Creek are not repenting of their philosophy of ministry; they are updating it. The last set of insights and methodologies did not 'work', but surely this new set will! At least that is what we are being told.

It should be mentioned that Willow Creek ought not to be shocked by the findings of their research. Critics of the seeker-sensitive movement have been pointing out these very flaws since the beginning. Time and again discerning Christian leaders have shown that the Willow model is unbiblical and incapable of developing truly biblical disciples of Christ. These critics have been ignored, ridiculed and vilified as negative, but their critique has proved true. Yet, rather than paying careful attention to these evaluations and swinging the movement back to a biblical pattern, Willow have consistently returned to their research to find answers, just as they are doing now.

The next step

The Willow Creek Association describes itself this way:

> We are driven by a calling to serve Christ-following leaders as they build biblically functioning churches — authentic, Acts 2 communities of faith that reach increasing numbers of lost people and grow them into fully devoted followers of Jesus Christ.[6]

With this as the stated goal we can empathize with Willow's 'earth-shaking' discovery that they have made a mistake. It is even ironic that those who have grown into 'fully devoted followers of Jesus Christ' are the very ones who are most disappointed with the Willow system and are thinking of leaving the churches.

We can see why Willow Creek's leadership wants to take out a clean sheet of paper and start all over again. One has to wonder, however, whether the sheet of paper is really that clean. Do the leaders have no agenda in mind? I think they do, and it is evident in their move towards the emergent church. For example, on 9-11 April 2008 the student ministry at Willow Creek offered a conference called Shift. Their advertisement brochure stated: 'As the world of student ministry continues to shift and change, so do the needs of those who serve students. Recognizing this, our team has designed an event that is unlike any other Student Ministries Conference we've ever hosted.'[7] The brochure promises to offer the students a variety of models of ministry at the conference. The fact is that it was heavily weighted towards mysticism and the emergent movement. Speakers included key emerging/emergent leaders Brian McLaren, Mark Yaconelli, Scot McKnight and Dan Kimball.[8]

Having discerned that the old way of the seeker-sensitive movement failed to produce the spiritual product they desired, Willow Creek are fast-forwarding to the newest wave that now promises what they did thirty years ago — 'authentic, Acts 2 communities of faith'.[9] This, however, is an even more tragic step, for while the seeker-sensitive movement has gone astray in many areas in its attempt to change the way we 'do' church, the majority within the movement at least paid lip service to the fundamentals of the faith. The emergent church, however, seeks not to change how we 'do' church, but to change the church itself by challenging the non-negotiable doctrines of the faith. Combining the emergent deconstructive philosophy with Willow Creek's influence and money could prove to be a powerful force for destruction. What may be written on this next 'clean sheet of paper' in the future is a far greater cause for concern than the one that is being thrown away today.

2

The Emergent Church Goes Ancient

Rumours are starting to circulate that the emergent church movement is running out of steam. After making the biggest splash and the most noise of anything in the Christian community for many years, it appears to be approaching exhaustion. Some, like Rob Bell and Erwin McManus, who are clearly in the 'emergent conversation', have denied their involvement. And people seem to be growing tired of hearing about postmodernism, its rejection of universal truth and its promotion of relativism. After all, how long can people live questioning the obvious and denying reality? These things play out nicely in philosophy classes and college coffee shops, but have serious limitations in the real world. Maybe it is time for the emergent ship to leave the dock and make way for the next fad.

As recently as January 2009, *Christianity Today* published a news article stating that 'One-time leaders of the emergent movement have recently distanced themselves from the term [and Emergent Village's board of directors has] eliminated the national coordinator position [held by Tony Jones].' *Christianity Today* commented that this move 'marked the latest sign that the movement is either decentralizing or disintegrating'.[1]

Additionally, several thinkers once associated with emergent, including pastor Dan Kimball and professor Scot McKnight, have formed a new network provisionally called Origins, dedicated to 'friends, pioneers, innovators, and catalysts who want to dream and work for the gospel together rather than alone'.[2]

But before we begin to make funeral arrangements for the emergent church it might be well to notice that it has not died; it is just in the process of metamorphosis. The emergent church has largely been a backlash against the seeker-sensitive movement, with its slick programs, high-octane entertainment and superficial worship. The postmodern generation wants something more authentic, something with substance, even something that is other-worldly. Where the seeker-sensitive movement attempted to make the church look like the world, emergent youth want a sense of the sacred. Where the seekers wanted to offer everything the world offered in purified form, the emergents want unique experiences the world does not have and cannot give. Where the seekers repudiated church history and behaved as though the church was born yesterday, the emergents want not only a link to the past, but a return to the past. These elements have always been present in the emergent movement, but are just now rising to the top of the agenda. It is not enough to complain about the modern church, or to brush aside all claims to truth as relative. Roots of some kind must anchor the movement if it is to last. What is it that will give this conversation a fixed point of reference and at the same time launch it into the next stage? It appears to be what some call 'Ancient-Future faith'.

Origins and leaders

The themes found in Ancient-Future faith have always been part of the emergent church, but are taking on additional weight as the movement matures. The term seems to have been coined by Robert Webber, who was a professor at Wheaton College and Northern Seminary. Webber wrote a number of works that are foundational to emergent philosophy, including *Ancient-Future Faith, Rethinking Evangelicalism for a Postmodern World* (published in 1999). *Christianity Today* calls Webber the 'Father of the ancient-future movement' and mentions the Robert E. Webber Center for an Ancient Evangelical Future which he founded.[3]

Chris Armstrong says the movement 'exploded in a 24-month period in 1977–1978, which saw the publication of Richard Foster's bestselling *Celebration of Discipline: The Path to Spiritual Growth* and Robert Webber's *Common Roots: A Call to Evangelical Maturity'*.[4] Armstrong documents other evangelical leaders during this same time period coming to similar conclusions, including Bethel College and Seminary president Carl Lundquist, Campus Crusade leader Peter Gillquist, Drew University's Tom Oden and theologians Donald Bloesch and Thomas Howard. The latter two were instrumental, along with Robert Webber, in penning *The Chicago Call: An Appeal to Evangelicals*, the prologue of which declared evangelicals' 'pressing need to reflect upon the substance of the biblical and historic faith and to recover the fullness of this heritage'.[5]

In 1982 *Christianity Today's* sister publication *Christian History* (now *Christian History & Biography*) began to encourage interest in church history and works of the Church Fathers (in itself a good thing). In 1988 Renovaré was founded by Richard Foster to introduce Roman Catholic mystics to Protestants and advance a mystical approach in evangelicalism.

We will explore later the content of Ancient-Future faith (subsequently referred to as 'A-F'), but for the present it would be helpful to know that a wide range of evangelicals now identify with it. In the February 2008 issue of *Christianity Today* several of its editors, including Mark Galli, David Neff, Ted Olson and Tim Morgan, have expressed their involvement with the movement. Anyone who has read *Christianity Today* in recent years will not be surprised to find its editors in sympathy with emergent-related views. Now they have clearly staked out their position.

Virtually all those involved with any aspect of the emergent conversation, as well as a growing number of more mainstream evangelical leaders, are embracing A-F practices and ideas. One Internet ministry, Lighthouse Trails (www.lighthousetrails.com), is dedicated to bringing to the awareness of Christians the vast number of evangelical leaders who are immersed, or at least dabbling, in mysticism, the principles of which A-F adherents embrace.

Stages of church history

As we attempt to understand A-F, we will start with the stages of church history through which Webber believes the church has travelled. This is important, for Webber informs us that 'You can best think about the future of the faith after you have gone back to the classical tradition.'[6] In other words, he is not trying to reinvent Christianity; he just wants to 'carry forward what the church has affirmed from its beginning'.[7] With this in mind, Webber looks back and sees six stages of church history: primitive (the first century); ancient or classical (100–600); medieval (600–1500); Reformation (1500–1750); modern (1750–1980), and post-modern (1980 to the present).[8] In Webber's view this final stage (postmodern) is a return to the second stage (ancient/classical), which he sees as the purest form of Christianity. He writes:

> It may be said broadly that the story of Christianity moves from a focus on mystery in the classical period, to institution in the medieval era, to individualism in the Reformation era, to reason in the modern era, and now, in the postmodern era, back to mystery.[9]

It is vital to note that the starting point for A-F is not the apostolic era of the first century, nor the New Testament documents. A-F does not return directly to Scripture for its practices and beliefs; it returns to the 'ancient' stage of the second to the seventh centuries. It would be unfair to say that Webber dismisses the apostolic age altogether, referring to it as 'primitive Christianity'. However, to grasp the issues it is necessary to realize that A-F advocates begin from a different point of reference from that of many evangelicals. They do not argue that their views in the areas of mysticism and ritual are based on New Testament teaching or example, for they cannot. This does not deter them, however, for they are reaching back to what they consider to be the 'rich' traditions and practices developed in the classical stage of church history. It is their contention that it was during this era that Christianity reached its zenith, and therefore for it to regain its spiritual health it is essential to return to the ancient stage, with its emphases and observances. The argument that we should look to the New Testament for our ecclesiastical model falls on deaf ears among the A-F community, for they are convinced that the richest expression of the Christian faith is not found in the Bible, but in the post-biblical early church. It is the desire of the A-F movement to mould the future church into the shape of the ancient church.

The wisdom of this attempt will be discussed later, but for now I want to mention some more recent phases of church history. Here we turn to modern evangelicalism of the last six decades. An article in *Christianity Today* summarizes Webber's threefold breakdown of evangelicalism since 1950 as found in his book *Younger Evangelicals*. Webber sees the years between 1950 and 1975 as the era of 'traditionals', who focused on doctrine, or, as he complains, 'being right': 'They poured their resources into Bible studies, Sunday school curricula, and apologetics materials.'[10] The traditionals were followed by the 'pragmatics', who ' "do" church growth, spawning the culturally engaged (and hugely successful) seeker-sensitive trend, with full-service megachurches and countless outreach programs'.[11] The pragmatics have been superseded by the 'younger evangelicals', who 'seek a Christianity that is "embodied" and "authentic" — distinctively Christian... The younger evangelicals seek a renewed encounter with a God beyond both doctrinal definitions and super-successful ministry programs.'[12]

While elements of all three types of evangelicals can be found today, according to Webber and *Christianity Today*, it is the younger, or emergent, evangelical that will dominate the twenty-first century and will represent the superior form of Christianity. Evangelicalism has finally grown up, having left behind the need for doctrinal correctness and outward success, and has evolved into the ancient faith of the early church. The church has returned full circle, and this is for the best — or so say the A-F people.

The Romans road

But exactly where is A-F taking the church? All signs point to Rome, or at least the suburbs of Rome. This is evidenced not only in the adoption of Rome's religious practices, or in embracing Catholic and Eastern Orthodox dogma (both subjects that we will cover below), but also in the direct statements and actions of those leading the movement. For example, there has been the steady trickle of noted evangelical leaders who have openly converted to Rome or Orthodoxy. We can think of Thomas Howard and Frank Schaeffer of some years back. I recently viewed a television program in which Frank Schaeffer (son of Francis Schaeffer) said he grew up being taught that Roman Catholicism was the 'whore of Babylon', but now he has seen the light and worships in an Orthodox church, has strong leanings towards Rome and finds little good to say about the Reformed theology of his father, or evangelicalism in general. More recently it has been the celebrated defection of the president of the Evangelical Theological Society, Francis Beckwith. Beckwith was willing to lay down his coveted position with ETS in order to join the Catholic Church. Indeed, some see no choice. John Henry Newman, of the old Oxford Movement (a mid-nineteenth century move towards Rome), stated, 'To read deeply in history is to cease being Protestant.'[13] And '...

at least some evangelicals have concluded that ... the only option left is to jump [the Protestant] ship.'[14]

Others do not want to go that far, but are open to a deeper ecumenicalism than in the past. Chris Armstrong, in his article for *Christianity Today*, summarizes:

> In short, the search for historic roots can and should lead not to conversion, but to a deepening ecumenical conversation, and a recognition by evangelicals that the Roman Catholics and Eastern Orthodox are fellow Christians with much to teach us.[15]

Apparently many agree with this sentiment. InterVarsity Press has released the *Ancient Christian Commentary* series to draw modern believers from across the spectrum of the Christian church back to the views of earlier church leaders. The 2007 Wheaton Theology Conference chose as its theme 'The Ancient Faith for the Church's Future'. As mentioned earlier, the editors of *Christianity Today* have come out as supporters of A-F. Even Liberty University observed the liturgical season of Lent. Thomas Nelson is currently publishing a series of eight books on 'The Ancient Practices', the first written by Brian McLaren, *Finding Our Way Again, the Return of the Ancient Practices*.[16] InterVarsity Press now has a whole division called *Formatio* dedicated to the promotion of 'spiritual formation' literature. *Formatio* boasts dozens of books written by authors such as Leighton Ford, Dallas Willard, Thomas Oden and Eugene Peterson.

The movement probably owes as much to Richard Foster as anyone. When Foster wrote his best-selling *Celebration of Discipline — The path to spiritual growth* in 1977 it hit the evangelical community like a bombshell. Here was a card-carrying evangelical (although a Quaker) urging believers to return to the mystical teachings of ancient Roman Catholicism to unearth the 'great treasures of spiritual reformation'. Foster introduced numerous mystics, most of them, but not all, from the monastic and Counter-Reformation periods, to modern evangelicals who had never heard of them. He then propounded that following the practices of these 'spiritual masters of the past' was essential to spiritual development. Since that time Foster and his many followers have flooded the evangelical community with mystical practices which promise a deeper level of spiritual life than anything witnessed since the Reformation disastrously (in their opinion) convinced believers of the doctrine of *sola Scriptura*. Since that time the race has been on to return Protestants to the 'mother church'.

The distinctions that have been recognized between conservative Protestant and Roman Catholic/Eastern Orthodox churches since Luther and Calvin are rapidly disappearing. The mood of the moment is not only that the three traditions can learn from each other, but that they can be reunited. How so? Certainly not through returning to the Bible, since 'doctrine divides'. But if we can put our doctrines on the back burner, seeing them as secondary issues at best, and return to the ancient practices and creeds, we can recognize our commonality in the ancient church. We will therefore be able to identify each other as brothers and sisters in Christ, despite insurmountable doctrinal differences. Unity between the major traditions will never be found as long as we adhere to our theological distinctives. But if we can lay these aside and unite over our experiences, common ancestors and ecumenical creeds, we revitalize the Christian faith.

It should be observed that most, if not all, of the moving is taking place from the Protestant side, not the Catholic/Orthodox side. This is because the A-F movement sees the Reformation as an unnecessary schism perpetrated by Protestants. Since it was the Protestants who split and went astray, it is necessary for them to come home. Of course some in the emergent conversation want to take this further and incorporate into the community those of other religions as well. But that is another story.

Monasticism

Hand in hand with the A-F movement is a revival in traditional monastic and religious orders. What is most interesting is that this resurgence is not unique to Christianity, or any particular branch of Christianity. A recent article in *U.S. News and World Report* documents Jewish, Islamic, Catholic and Protestant interest in more traditional and liturgical forms of worship, especially among young adults.[17] But an almost inexplicable aspect of all this is an attraction to monastic practices. The term 'new monasticism' is becoming common on the Internet and among emergent and mystical-oriented writers such as Richard Foster, Tony Jones and Brian McLaren. The Winter 2007 issue of *Christian History and Biography* is devoted to the monasticism of sixth-century monk St Benedict and states, 'No topic touches young evangelical students more than monasticism.'[18] Why would this be true? On the one hand, the fragmented, success-oriented, materialistic age is running out of steam for many. Something more is needed — something with depth, something beyond the superficial entertainment-focused Christian tradition that many have grown up with. On the other hand, there has been a whole line of books (from the writings of Richard Foster, to Kathleen Norris's *The Cloister Walk*, to Eugene Peterson's *Eat This Book*) leading to numerous promotions of *lectio divina* (a unique approach to reading Scripture that I will discuss later) and contemplative prayer, and to the general rise of mysticism and the emergent church which has pushed these concepts into the minds of young people.

Between the combination of restlessness and disillusionment and the promise of better things in solitude, asceticism and a life of spiritual discipline, monasticism has a certain draw. To be sure, this is a 'new monasticism' with a twenty-first-century twist. The origin of early Christian monasticism came in the fourth century following the legalization of Christianity:

[Until then martyrdom was] the ultimate test of devotion [but at that point] ... the Christian ascetic inherited the mantle of the martyr [becoming a sort of living martyr]... Monks sought to live an angelic life on earth, neither marrying nor having children. By refusing to participate in the continual process of physically repopulating the earth, they recognized that Christ's coming had initiated a new age and believed that their lives could help usher in his kingdom.[19]

Contemporary young people attracted to monasticism are not likely to abandon conventional life and live as hermits in caves, or even monasteries. They are more likely to continue to keep their jobs, live in standard dwellings with family or friends and carry out the normal activities of modern society. However, they are yearning for some sense of serenity, for quiet and simpler times, and therein lies the pull of monastic and ancient practices. But are these things the panacea they crave and, more importantly, are they biblical? Let's take a closer look.

Ancient-Future practices

In a recent sermon dealing with the emergent/emerging church, Mark Driscoll, pastor of Mars Hill in Seattle and a self-described emerging church leader, identified four lanes in which the emergent/emerging movement is travelling:

1. In the first lane are *emerging evangelicals who believe in basic Christian doctrine*, such as the Bible being God's Word and Jesus dying for our sins. They also tend to form the 'hip, cool church', according to Driscoll. Pastors who may fall in this category include Dan Kimball and Donald Miller. Without taking much time to debate with Driscoll at this point, I would certainly challenge the notion that Donald Miller is a supporter of basic Christian doctrine. Kimball, on the other hand, does hold to certain doctrinal positions such as the three ancient ecumenical creeds, but would not want to drift much beyond them.

2. Travelling down the second lane are the *house-church evangelicals* who are doctrinally Christian brothers and sisters, Driscoll says. They do not support creating large churches and instead form little house churches, or churches in other smaller settings such as coffee shops.

3. Driscoll places himself and Mars Hill in the third lane, which he calls *'Emerging reformers'*, who believe in all of the evangelical distinctives and embrace Reformed theological traditions. Emerging reformers also try to find ways to make the church relevant, accessible and culturally connected; they tend to be charismatic and many are involved in church planting.

4. In the fourth lane is a group of *emergent liberals* which, Driscoll feels, has 'totally gotten off the highway and is lost out in the woods'. Although Driscoll was initially connected to this group, which also tries to find innovative ways to 'do church', he left, citing the reason that they call into question many parts of the 'Christian doctrine'. Some of their questions include: 'Do you need Jesus to go to heaven?' 'Is anybody really going to hell?' 'Is sex outside of marriage, including homosexuality, sinful?' Leaders in this lane include Brian McLaren and Rob Bell.[20]

The reader can see how fragmented and complicated the emergent conversation has become. Like most movements, as it matures it has changed form and is becoming increasingly difficult to define. Many, in all of Driscoll's four lanes, are distancing themselves from the emergent label itself since it has become somewhat pejorative. What all lanes of the emergent, or emerging, movement have in common is the desire to be relevant to the postmodern culture. Some have sacrificed the faith in this effort; others have been more biblically sound. But out of this 'junk-drawer category' (as Driscoll calls it) I see springing the Ancient-Future faith emphasis which is common to most of those in all of the emergent/emerging lanes. This is the belief that the purest expression of Christianity was found in the ancient period of church history (100–600) and that it is to this era that we must return.

What is so special and inviting to emerging Christians about these early years of Christianity? It was during this era that the early church rituals, traditions and liturgies were developed, and it was a time during which mystical practices began to define spirituality and close encounters with God. This is the era of church history which many believe we must appropriate to our own times if we are to experience authentic Christianity. Let's take a look at some of the specific practices which are returning to favour through the A-F resurgence.

Lectio divina

This term and practice is increasingly cropping up in evangelical circles. Many, having been told that *lectio divina* is nothing but a devotional, contemplative reading of Scripture, have been little concerned, but we should look deeper. According to *Wikipedia*:

> *Lectio divina* is Latin for *divine reading*, spiritual reading, or 'holy reading', and represents a method of prayer and scriptural reading intended to engender communion with the Tri-une God and to increase in the knowledge of God's Word. It is a way of praying with Scripture that calls one to study, ponder, listen and, finally, pray from God's Word.[21]

Given this benign definition, one could be justified in asking, 'What is wrong with slowly reading and meditating on Scripture?' Scriptural meditation has been practised and prescribed throughout biblical times to the present. Eugene Peterson (author of many evangelical books and the paraphrase *The Message*) published *Eat This Book* in 2006 to promote *lectio divina*. Peterson writes:

> *Lectio divina* is not a methodical technique for reading the Bible. It is a cultivated, developed habit of *living* the text in Jesus's name. This is the way, the *only* way that the Holy

Scriptures become formative in the Christian church and become salt and leaven in the world.[22]

If *lectio divina* is in fact the *only way* that the Scriptures become formative in the church and the *only way* they become salt and leaven in the world, as Peterson claims, it would be wise for us to understand and become practitioners of *lectio divina*. But a closer look reveals the opposite. *Lectio divina* can be traced back as far as Origen (AD 220). Various monastic rules have practised *lectio divina*, most notably those of Benedict and Ignatius of Loyola, although twelfth-century monk Guigo II is credited with systematizing the method as it is currently used today. Pope Benedict XVI recently recommended its use as a means of promoting spiritual formation.

Mark Yaconelli, a strong proponent of this ancient tradition, tells us, 'When we engage in *lectio divina*, we are *not seeking to read the Bible for knowledge or instruction* (although both of those may come), nor are we seeking the escape of a good story. Instead we come to the words of the Bible seeking to be with God' (emphasis mine).[23] Ken Boa, another promoter of mystical Christianity, explains that *lectio divina* involves four movements:[24]

Reading (Lectio)

Since *lectio divina* engages the whole person, your bodily posture is important. A seated position that is erect but not tense or slouched is best... Remember that unlike ordinary reading, in *lectio* you are seeking to be *shaped* by the Word more than *informed* by the Word [emphasis his].[25]

Meditation (Meditatio)

'Meditation is a spiritual work of holy desire and an interior invitation for the Spirit to pray and speak within us (Romans 8:26-27)... Meditation will do you little good if you try to control the outcome.'[26] Incorporating the Spiritual Exercises of Ignatius of Loyola (see below) is recommended for meditation.

Prayer (Oratio)

Boa informs us that 'Oratio [Prayer] is a time for participation in the interpenetrating subjectivity of the Trinity through prolonged mutual presence and growing identification with the life of Christ.'[27]

Contemplation (Contemplatio)

To the uninitiated, contemplation is often confused with meditation, but they are not the same. In ordinary circles meditation describes deep thinking and analysing with a rational mind, and some may use 'contemplation' as a synonym for this activity. But in mystical circles contemplation is:

> ... a theological grace that cannot be reduced to logical, psychological, or aesthetic categories... It is best for us to stop talking and 'listen to Him' in simple and loving attentiveness. In this strange and holy land we must remove the sandals of our ideas, constructs and inclinations, and quietly listen for the voice of God. [28]

Yaconelli tells us that one technique to help in this process is to take a word or phrase (in essence a mantra) and 'repeat it to yourself, allowing the rest of the text to fall away. As you prayerfully repeat it, different thoughts, feelings, and images may arise...' By this methodology we can 'pray ourselves empty' and '[you] sink into God beneath all your thoughts and feelings'.[29]

As can easily be seen, lectio divina is not a devotional method of Scripture reading, but a highly mystical approach. The reader does not encounter Scripture in order to grasp the understanding of what God has communicated to us and apply it. Instead, a super-rational experience is sought in which God speaks to an individual beyond the written page in imaginative and non-cognitive ways.

It is also instructive to note that this method of Bible reading is not drawn from the Scriptures themselves, but from medieval monks during a period of time when the church of Rome was abandoning the clear understanding of the Word of God and seeking alternatives. The Ancient-Future faith movement is not going back to Scripture for its teachings, but to the practices and traditions of men.

Divine Office and the new monasticism

The best-known of the monastic rules is that of Benedict. Benedict's Rule, which is receiving renewed attention today (see *Christian History & Biography*, Winter 2007), was written for sixth-century monks who entered Benedict's monastery with the goal of hearing from God. The first word of Benedict's Rule is: 'Listen.' So Benedict structured each day around two activities which were designed for listening to the voice of God. Four hours a day were devoted to the *lectio divina* and four hours were spent in the 'Divine Office'. The Divine Office consisted of praying over the 150 psalms each week, plus other readings from Scripture, writings of Christian authors, hymns and prayers. The Divine Office is comprised of eight set times of prayer (one nocturnal and seven daytime offices) in which certain prayers are recited.

Robert Benson, author of *In Constant Prayer* (which is part of Thomas Nelson's 'The Ancient Practices' series), assures us that the Divine Office reaches back to the beginning of the human race, has been practised by the people of God ever since and is even being prayed by Jesus to the Father at this time.[30]

In fact, the Divine Office, as practised throughout church history, is the product of men's imagination, not an inspired mandate from God. Our Lord has certainly called us to be people devoted to prayer, but he neither gives us, nor demands from us, a prescribed set of prayers to be recited by rote at set times of the day.

Until recently few outside of the Roman Catholic clergy paid much attention to the Divine Office, but there has been a renewed interest in such things swirling around the 'new monasticism'. The older form of monasticism and religious orders has been on the decline for a long time. The number of men in such orders has declined by 46% in Europe and 30% in America since 1978.[31] 'Yet most suggest that new and powerful forms of the monastic impulse may even now be arising.'[32] These new forms, found in both Protestant and Catholic circles, consist of those who have connected themselves to some aspect of monastic living while remaining in the world. What we are finding is an increasing attraction, especially among young people, to incorporate these ancient practices into their lives. Perhaps, as the world speeds up and disappoints, there is a draw to a connection with the past when things were seemingly slower and less complicated.

'Spiritual Exercises'

Eugene Peterson tells us, 'Ignatius of Loyola's *Spiritual Exercises* is one of the most influential guidebooks for directing us in listening.'[33] Gregory Boyd goes further: 'I and many others have found Ignatius's *Spiritual Exercises* to be the most powerful tool for helping us grow in our walk with God.'[34] These are powerful endorsements by well-known evangelical spokesmen.

Ignatius was a Roman Catholic monk during the time of the Counter-Reformation of the sixteenth century. He is known today primarily as the founder of the Society of Jesus, or the Jesuits, and for his *Spiritual Exercises*. The 'Spiritual Exercises' are a method of contemplative meditations. According to the Jesuits' website:

> The Spiritual Exercises of St. Ignatius of Loyola are a month-long program of meditations, prayers, considerations, and contemplative practices that help Catholic faith become more fully alive in the everyday life of contemporary people. It is set out in a brief manual or handbook: sparse, taciturn,

and practical. It presents a formulation of Ignatius' spirituality in a series of prayer exercises, thought experiments, and examinations of consciousness — designed to help a retreatant (usually with the aid of a spiritual director) to experience a deeper conversion into life with God in Christ, to allow our personal stories to be interpreted by being subsumed in a Story of God.[35]

The Spiritual Exercises are basically a means to expedite the experience of classical mysticism. Mysticism, as found in Eastern forms, the Kabbalah (Jewish), New Age, or Roman Catholicism, all follow the same pattern: purgation, illumination and union. *Purgation* is an emptying of ourselves, and so the purpose of the first Ignatian movement is to create 'a space within us that the Lord can fill'.[36] In *illumination* we are filled up with images of God, which is accomplished in the exercises 'by imaginatively contemplating scenes in the four Gospels'.[37] Through these practices unmediated *union with God* is supposedly accomplished, which is the goal of the exercises. Ignatius's exercises are now being adapted for use by Protestants in books such as *Sacred Listening* by James L. Wakefield and promoted heavily by everyone from Richard Foster to Eugene Peterson.

Liturgical worship

James K. A. Smith, author of *Who's Afraid of Postmodernism?*, informs us that postmodern religion will be liturgical in nature, for '… the rhythms of ritual and liturgy are gracious practices that enable discipleship and formation… Properly postmodern worship reclaims the holistic, full-orbed materiality of liturgical worship that activates all the senses.'[38] With this concept as foundational, there is a wholesale rush to liturgical practices which originated in Roman Catholicism and Eastern Orthodoxy. Although not found in Scripture, practices such as the rosary, prayer ropes, Stations of the Cross, icons, incense, making the sign of the cross, use of crucifixes, labyrinths, Benedictine chants,[39] and more, are encouraged as forms of worship in the A-F church.

As can easily be seen, there is a major push for ancient (but not New Testament) liturgical practices in order to anchor the A-F faith of the emergent church. All of this takes the adherents a step back towards Rome and Orthodoxy on a practical basis. But what about beliefs? What does the A-F movement believe?

Ancient-Future beliefs

In his book *Finding Our Way Again — The return of the ancient practices,* Brian McLaren, the most recognizable name in the emergent church movement, signals a shift, or at least a new emphasis, within the movement towards ancient practices from earlier periods of church history. As usual, McLaren believes the church has lost its way as a result of its refusal to follow God's leading. The church has become 'proud and unteachable', but, fortunately, a few 'humble and teachable' people (guess who?) are pointing out the right path:[40] 'When the community of faith realizes it has lost its way, it begins looking forward by looking back... It looks to its ancient practices to help it reset its future course.'[41]

This means that the church, in order to find its way again, must look to and adopt the early church (not New Testament church) traditions and rituals, especially the 'seven ancient practices' of fasting, pilgrimage, common daily prayers, a weekly day of rest, annual holy days and seasons, tithing and the observance of a sacred meal, as they find fulfilment in the 'threefold way' of purgation, illumination and union with God.[42] What seems to have precipitated this renewed interest in ancient practices and mysticism is recognition that the emergent movement is in need of roots. McLaren writes, 'More and more of us feel, more and more intensely, the need for a fresh creative alternative — a fourth alternative, something beyond militarist scientific secularism, pushy religious fundamentalism, and mushy amorphous spirituality.'[43] I assume by these strong remarks McLaren means that the emergent church, having already rejected modern evangelicalism and fundamentalism, must now move beyond an 'amorphous spirituality' and put down some anchors. These anchors are sinking into the soil of ancient spiritual practices.[44]

Finding Our Way Again is actually the introductory volume in *The Ancient Practices Series* composed of eight titles published by Thomas Nelson and edited by Phyllis Tickle. The other seven works will each develop one of the seven ancient practices deemed important for the emerging church. It would seem that this series of books marks the official marriage of the Ancient-Future faith movement with the emergent movement. These two have been seen flirting in various places, but it appears that the union has now been consummated.

So far we have looked at the origins, leaders, basic ideas and practices of the Ancient-Future faith paradigm; we need to press on now to an examination of the underlying beliefs within the movement. What will be documented is that this system, claiming evangelical roots, is, by and large, in line with the doctrine of Roman Catholicism and Eastern Orthodoxy rather than biblical truth.

An Enlightenment backlash

As with most material related to the emergent church, the Enlightenment is depicted as the great evil of modern times, and postmodernity as the welcomed rescuer from Enlightenment thought. Then, even though the true evangelical church has always opposed many Enlightenment teachings, it is nevertheless painted as the loyal slave of the Enlightenment. Robert Webber provides one of the clearest presentations:

> This Enlightenment paradigm produced three convictions shared equally by Christians and non-Christians: foundationalism, structuralism, and the notion of metanarrative.

Foundationalism is 'the philosophical theological conviction that there are beliefs or experiences that are in themselves beyond doubt and upon which systems of belief and understanding can therefore be constructed with certainty'. Structuralism is the belief that societies construct texts to make meaning out of life and that the meaning which is in the text can be commonly agreed upon by its interpreters through the use of reason. The metanarrative consists of the stories of the text. These stories make sense out of life by providing an interpretation of the world from its beginning to its end.[45]

While this is not the place to carry on a philosophical debate with Enlightenment theory and influence, suffice it to say that postmodern Christianity (emergent and A-F) rejects all three convictions. Of course, evangelicalism also rejected the secularized form of these convictions. For example, evangelicals did not accept the idea that truth can be found with certainty through reason alone and, therefore, always subjected reason to the revelation of Scripture. But evangelicals have believed that the revelation of God (the Word) could be understood through reason and proper interpretative tools (hermeneutics) resulting in foundational truth. This is rejected by the postmodern church, which would say that (at least most) truth cannot be known with certainty, and therefore the views of evangelicals of the past, shaped as they claim by the Enlightenment, do not relate to the postmodern culture. Webber asks, 'Where do we go to find a Christianity that speaks meaningfully to a postmodern world?' His answer is that 'The classical tradition [the second to the seventh centuries] appears to be the most productive... Therefore, our challenge is not to reinvent Christianity, but to restore and then adapt classical Christianity to the postmodern cultural situation.'[46]

The rule of faith

Webber does not himself make a complete break with the Enlightenment, believing that the metanarrative of Christianity is the correct one,[47] however limited. And many within the A-F movement would accept a level of certainty as found in the so-called 'rule of faith'. This rule 'was regarded as a summary of the most important features of the Christian faith, a framework for the essential truths confessed by those who stood in the tradition of apostolic teachings'.[48] The problem lies in determining the content of the 'rule of faith'. According to Webber, a number of rules of faith began to be put forward in early church history in attempts to define Christian teachings in the light of various heresies, such as Gnosticism. 'Eventually, the rule of faith became universally summarized in the Apostles' Creed,'[49] which is 'the end-product of the gradual development of Western creeds... Today's version dates from the sixth or seventh century.'[50]

The Apostles' Creed, in its general summary of Christian thought, is limited in scope, however, so between AD 300 and 500 the universal church formulated two other 'ecumenical creeds' to explain what it believed. These were the Nicene Creed (begun at the Council of Nicaea in 325, but actually formulated at the Council of Constantinople in 381), and the Chalcedonian Creed in 451. Between these three creeds a number of doctrines were established as orthodox, including the deity of the Son (Nicene), the Trinity (Nicene) and the two natures of Christ (Chalcedonian). According to the A-F understanding, other confessions and statements of faith have been developed over the years that express the belief of particular groups or denominations, but none of these carries the weight of the three ecumenical creeds. As a result A-F thinkers believe the church can be certain of the doctrines expressed in the creeds, but must be willing to compromise on all other points of theology. Webber writes:

> We need to recognize that confessions do not meet the criteria of universality, antiquity, and consensus... Their value is not for the whole church, but for a part of the church... These confessions are all secondary to the creeds and are not binding upon the whole church.[51]

Unfortunately for Webber's view, even the three 'ecumenical creeds' have not received 'universality and consensus'. According to church historian Tony Lane, the Apostles' Creed 'has always enjoyed wide acceptance in the West... [But] it has never been in general use in the Eastern Church, though it is treated with respect.'[52] Concerning the Chalcedonian Creed Lane writes, 'The emperor intended this document to cement unity with the Eastern Church. Its effect was more like dynamite than cement. Egypt and other areas have never accepted Chalcedon to this day.'[53] The Nicene Creed has been the most ecumenical of the creeds, but even here the East and West differ in one important area: 'In the East the belief was and is that the Holy Spirit proceeds from the Father *through* the Son. In the West, however, the belief grew that the Holy Spirit proceeds from the Father *and* the Son' (emphasis his).[54] While this might seem a matter of little importance to us today, it would be a major factor in 1054, bringing about the Great Schism which became the final dividing point between the Eastern Orthodox Church and the Western Roman Catholic Church.

So much for A-F's belief in the 'universality and consensus' of the ecumenical creeds. The fact is that even these creeds have never been given a universal consensus by the whole church. The finger is often pointed at the Protestant church for its lack of unity and many doctrinal distinctions, but Rome and Orthodoxy have to be hypocritical to do so. Webber is either being somewhat naïve or is perhaps ill-informed when he writes, 'I sense that evangelicals in the postmodern world need to affirm what the church has always believed, *everywhere and by all,* and give great authority to the common tradition and less weight to the theology of a particular tradition' (emphasis mine).[55]

Non-credal doctrines

In the A-F system what is to be done with other important doctrines that fall outside the boundaries of the three ecumenical creeds? In essence they are non-binding and unimportant and therefore open to compromise. Take the crucial doctrine of salvation. After all, what could be more essential than one's eternal destiny? Yet concerning the doctrine of salvation no universal creed has been written, and therefore how one becomes a Christian is wide open to debate. Webber writes:

> Although the entire church is united in its belief that all are sinners and that Jesus Christ's death and resurrection procure salvation, there exists a number of explanations about our sinful nature and the means of receiving the benefits of Christ's death.[56]

No wonder Brian McLaren states, 'I don't think we've got the gospel right yet. What does it mean to be "saved"? When I read the Bible, I don't see it meaning, "I'm going to heaven after I die."... None of us has arrived at orthodoxy.'[57]

This does not mean that A-F has no concept of a gospel. As is predictable, A-F reaches back to the 'ancient' church, rather than Scripture, for a gospel message. Webber writes, 'Evangelism in the early church was associated with the victory of Christ over evil and the establishment of the kingdom of God.'[58] He then turns to a third-century ritual in which an individual is taken through a number of stages, lasting up to three years and leading to baptism and entrance into the church.[59] What is most instructive is that this tradition is not taught or found in the New Testament, but some 300 years later. It is typical of A-F to reach back to the traditions of men rather than the inspired text of Scripture. This takes us to A-F's understanding of the Bible.

Scripture

Webber writes, 'A new feature of evangelicals in the postmodern world is the growing awareness that the Bible, which takes us to Christ, belongs to the church. The church preceded Scripture in time.'[60] As can be seen, the A-F movement rejects the *sola Scriptura* position of the Reformers and adopts Rome's view in regard to authority. The church presides over Scripture — in the final analysis authority rests in the church.

How this actually works out is more involved. Which church, for example, has the final word — Rome, the Orthodox churches, Lutherans, etc.? Webber never really answers this, but seems to be looking towards Rome. And what role do tradition and the pronouncements of the Church Fathers and the ancient councils play? Webber's response to this question is most interesting:

> Any writing of a Father of the church, or any council or assembly of the church that stood in the apostolic tradition, was an extension of the principle of inspiration. Therefore, while the apostles were the original authority of inspiration, a writing of Augustine or another Father of the church, or a creed or council that extended or expounded an idea in keeping with apostolic teaching enjoyed a kind of apostolic authority. Because the church was viewed as the one true interpreter of the faith, the authority of the church grew greater and greater through time... Finally, the church established a magisterium for the proper interpretation of truth and positioned the Pope as the true spokesperson of truth.[61]

As might be expected, placing final authority in the pope did not go down well with everyone and paved the way for the Reformation in which the Reformers rejected the authority of the pope and the Roman Catholic Church and placed it in Scripture alone. Webber reacts to this: 'The Reformers pulled Scripture away from the church, separated it from tradition, and set it over against popes and councils, and made it stand on its own.'[62]

Webber summarizes well the A-F position:

> The postmodern challenge to authority is best met, not by returning to *sola scriptura*, nor by the modern evangelical defense of the Bible, but by returning to the origins of authority in

the Christian faith. The church possesses, interprets, guards, and hands down the truth.[63]

Mysticism

As with other streams within the emergent movement, there is a keen interest in mysticism. Webber highly recommends reading the so-called 'spiritual classics' that Richard Foster has introduced to the Protestant church. This includes mystics such as Meister Eckhart, Teresa of Avila, John of the Cross, George Fox, William Law and Thomas Merton. Webber concludes: 'The value of all these books is indispensable to spirituality. Those who neglect these works do so to their harm, and those who read them do so for their inspiration and spiritual growth.'[64]

McLaren devotes three chapters in his book *Finding Our Way Out* to the 'threefold way' of purgation, illumination and union, which is common to all forms of mysticism, Christian or otherwise. However, McLaren does not describe the 'threefold way' as his mentors and the ancient mystics (such as St John of the Cross and Teresa of Avila) do. He either does not understand his subject (which is highly unlikely), or he is using his winsome pen to make these approaches much more attractive than they would normally be for many people. But he definitely promotes contemplation (a mystical form of prayer), *lectio divina* (a mystical form of Scripture reading) and the daily office (a ritualistic form of prayer).[65]

The ancient mystics, to whom the movement looks, were not afraid to state their case. For example, in his famous work *Dark Night of the Soul*, St John of the Cross informs his reader that the first stage of the 'threefold way', that of purgation, is a stage in which the senses, affections and intellect are all purged or killed. He writes:

When, therefore, the four passions of the soul — which are joy, grief, hope and fear — are calmed through continual mortification; when the natural desires have been lulled to sleep

> ... by means of habitual times of aridity; and when the har-
> mony of the senses and the interior faculties causes a sus-
> pension of labour and a cessation from the work of meditation
> ... these enemies cannot obstruct this spiritual liberty...[66]

The purpose behind the deadening of our senses is in order that they should not hinder the way of the spirit: 'The reason for this is that the soul is now becoming alien and remote from common sense and knowledge of things, in order that, being annihilated in this respect it may be informed with the Divine.'[67]

Teresa of Avila, in her *Interior Castle*, concurs, 'The person who does most is he who thinks least and desires to do least.'[68] This is because the whole goal of mysticism is to experience something in a super-rational way. Teresa writes:

> It is quite a common experience in such cases for the under-
> standing to be less apt for meditation. I think the reason
> must be that the whole aim of meditation is to seek God, and
> once He is found, and the soul grows accustomed to seeking
> Him again by means of the will, it has no desire to fatigue
> itself with intellectual labour.[69]

The goal of mysticism is to purge the senses and intellect in order to be filled up with a form of illumination that bypasses the mind and leads to an inexplicable experience of ecstasy which culminates in union with God. The 'threefold way' is never taught in Scripture, but is a vital component of A-F and the emergent church.

Conclusion

Although A-F is a move back towards Rome, rather than a move back towards Scripture, Chris Armstrong, associate professor of church history at Bethel Seminary, assures us that it is none other than the Lord who is leading this parade:

That more and more evangelicals have set out upon it is reason for hope for the future of gospel Christianity. That they are receiving good guidance on this road from wise teachers is reason to believe that Christ is guiding the process. And that they are meeting and learning from fellow Christians in the other two great confessions, Roman Catholic and Eastern Orthodox, is reason to rejoice in the power of love.[70]

Armstrong's optimism is without biblical support. He is making a classical mistake based upon his apparently postmodern worldview: that truth emerges from, and can be verified by, our experience. If something seems to be working out (as per our subjective observations) it must be of God. The scriptural position is that truth emerges from, and can be verified by, God's Word, regardless of what our experience might be. The mere fact that the major branches of Christendom are locking arms does not prove that 'Christ is guiding the process'. It may be the very opposite, which I believe to be the case.

3

Invasion of Paganism

Have you heard *The Secret*? For a short time it was all the rage throughout American society and it has even infiltrated the church. From daytime talk shows to the business world, *The Secret* (presented in both book and DVD forms) made an impact. The inspiration behind *The Secret* came in 2004 when an old book called *The Science of Getting Rich* was placed in the hands of Rhonda Byrne. Byrne was going through a difficult period in her life and the message in this book rejuvenated her imagination. Over the course of the next two months Byrne claims to have read 'hundreds' of books and studied the lives of great leaders in history. She discovered, or so she maintains, that many great names from the past (e.g. Churchill, Einstein, Emerson), as well as the present (e.g. Jack Canfield, author and co-creator of the best-selling *Chicken Soup for the Soul* series), were aware of the information found in *The Secret*. In the past, those in the know kept this information to themselves. Byrne, however, wanted to disseminate what she had learned to the masses. Thus began her new mission in life — to spread the knowledge she had discovered to the ends of the earth. And so began the journey of *The Secret*.

The Secret, written by Ms Byrne, has been one of the fastest-selling books in history. As early as 8 May 2007, it had sold 5.3 million copies and its publisher, Atria, says that it was selling 150,000 per week. In addition there is a web-based, video-on-demand version (also available on DVD). Premiering in March 2006, the DVD sold 1.5 million copies within a few months. (You can watch the first twenty-four minutes of the DVD online for free at You Tube). Of course, it did not hurt Byrne's cause when Oprah Winfrey dedicated a two-hour show to the project, and announced that she had been using *The Secret* all her life without knowing it.

Just as *The Secret* began to fade in popularity, Oprah, who has perhaps become the best-known cheerleader for New Age spirituality in recent years, introduced Eckhart Tolle and his book *A New Earth — Awakening to Your Life's Purpose*. Tolle clearly states that the purpose of his book is 'to bring about a shift in consciousness, that is to say, awaken'.[1] Awakening, for those unfamiliar with the language of the 'new spirituality', is 'a shift in consciousness in which thinking and awareness separate'.[2] Tolle, in line with most Eastern thought, believes that all things are one with the universe[3] (a concept known as monism). This Eastern pantheistic teaching ultimately leads to all things being God. True to form, in *A New Earth,* Tolle wants us to know that 'we are light',[4] we are 'I Am',[5] we are 'the Truth'[6] and 'we are God'.[7]

While most evangelicals can see the fallacy of *The Secret* and *The New Earth*, when the ideas are packaged more carefully, and less directly, not all are so discerning. For example, this Eastern form of spirituality has infiltrated the church, at least subtly, through the wildly popular novel *The Shack*, written by William Young. In this piece of fiction the very essence of God is challenged when Young, quoting from Unitarian-Universalist Buckminster Fuller, declares God to be a verb, not a noun.[8] In a related statement, Young has Jesus say of the Holy Spirit, 'She is Creativity; she is Action; she is Breathing of Life.'[9] Yet the Bible presents God as a person (a noun), not an action (a verb); not as creativity, but as a person. When this truth is denied we are moving from the biblical understanding of a personal God to an Eastern understanding of God in everything.[10] Thus we are not surprised that, when Mack (the main character in the novel) asks whether he will see his dead daughter Missy again, he is told, 'Of course, you might see

me in a piece of art, or music, or silence, or through people, or in
creation, or in your joy and sorrow.'[11] This is not biblical teaching.
This idea seems to be repeated in a line from a song Missy creates:
'Come, kiss me, wind, and take my breath till you and I are one.'[12]
At what point do we become one with creation? Again, this is an
Eastern concept, not a biblical one.

Young reinforces his Eastern leanings with a statement right out
of New Age (or 'new spirituality') teachings: Papa (the God-figure
in the book) tells Missy's father, 'Just say it out loud. There is
power in what my children declare.'[13] Rhonda Byrne would echo
this idea in her book, *The Secret*, but you will not find it in the
Bible. Jesus even tells Mack that 'God, who is the ground of all
being, dwells in, around, and through all things — ultimately
emerging as the real.'[14] This is pure New Age spirituality and it
seems to be invading the evangelical church with regularity.

In order to understand what is at stake, I want to deal directly
with the teachings of *The Secret* as a representative of why and
how this invasion of paganism has become a challenge to God's
people. By examining the teachings of *The Secret* I believe we will
get a good flavour of the kinds of things that paganism is using to
entice people to its worldview.

What is it?

At the heart of *The Secret* is the 'law of attraction', which is,
simply stated, that our thoughts control the universe. Through the
law of attraction we obtain the fulfilment of our desires. When we
know what we want, we simply believe it will happen and see
ourselves in abundance, and we will attract it: 'It works every time,
with every person.'[15]

The 'experts' in *The Secret* DVD and book assure us that 'The
law of attraction is really obedient.' They claim that:

[It is] like having the universe as your catalogue and you flip
through it and go, 'Well, I'd like to have this experience, and

I'd like to have that product, and I'd like to have a person like that.' ... It is you just placing your order with the universe. It's really that easy.

How does the law of attraction work? It all goes back to your mind: 'What you think about you bring about. Your life is a physical manifestation of the thoughts that go on in your head.' The theory is that like attracts like; therefore everything in your life is what you attract, good or bad.

Since we have thousands of thoughts every day (up to 60,000, we are told), how do we know what we are attracting? After all, it is impossible to attract every single thing that passes through our minds. The key lies not just in our minds, but our feelings. It is our feelings which let us know what we are attracting to our lives: 'If you are feeling good your future is on track with what you are desiring. When you are feeling bad you are creating a future which is off track with your desires.'

It is highly important, then, to be in touch with your feelings because, 'Whatever you're thinking and feeling today is creating your future. And you are getting exactly what you are feeling about, not so much what you are thinking about.'

This would be a good point at which to distinguish general optimism and positive thinking from the message of *The Secret*. Most people would agree that our outlook on life will have a profound impact on how we live. Those who are enthusiastic about life, highly motivated and excited about the prospects in front of them are likely to accomplish much more, and do so with much more joy, than those who simply endure, or even dread, their existence. I think it could be generally agreed that our thought lives can have a real effect on our health. While the jury is still out on this, some studies have concluded that tension, dread, grief, depression and anxiety are major factors in certain illnesses. But that is not the same as saying that our thoughts 'create' the future. Our thoughts will, to a large extent, contribute to how we feel and together they may affect the future, but they do not produce 'exactly' what we think and feel.

Scripture also places huge importance on the mind — how we think and what we think about is crucial. As Christians we know it is through the 'renewing of [our minds]' that our lives are transformed (Rom. 12:2). We are told to take 'every thought captive to the obedience of Christ' (2 Cor. 10:5), meaning that every philosophy and belief which runs counter to the truth of God's Word must be challenged and defeated lest it conform our thinking and lifestyle to those of the world. It is for these reasons that Paul admonishes us to think, or dwell on, the things which are true, honourable, right, pure, lovely, of good repute, excellent and worthy of praise (Phil. 4:8). This is not a call to 'positive thinking', but to biblical thinking. So Scripture does not deny the role of the mind in shaping our lives; it elevates the mind's role. But it also limits it. Our thoughts have power, but not all power. They affect, but they do not create or determine. Ultimate power, creation and destiny lie in the hands of God, not in the minds of people. Positive thinking has blurred these lines for years, but *The Secret* erases the lines and with them all doubt. With *The Secret* we are the final arbitrators, judges and determiners. Our futures are in our hands — God is eliminated altogether, or at best manipulated.

How to use it

The Secret offers a three-step plan to mastering the universe:

> *Step 1 — Ask.* Make a command to the universe. The universe responds to your thoughts: 'It is just like placing your order with the universe. It is really that easy.'
>
> *Step 2 — Believe.* Believe that it is already yours, 'and the universe will start rearranging itself to make it happen for you'.
>
> *Step 3 — Receive.* 'Begin to feel wonderful about it, feel the way you will feel once it arrives; feel it now.'

The problem with implementing these simple steps, Byrne informs us, is that we have not thought in this way in the past. So how do we change our thinking so that we can begin to attract the things we want? There are two important components.

First, we are to *'be grateful'*. When you are grateful you will start to attract more of the good things you want. Without question gratefulness is a characteristic that is right and biblical. However, gratefulness in *The Secret's* system is merely a manipulative tool to pressurize the universe into giving us more — more of what we want.

The second component is to *visualize*: 'When you visualize you materialize.' In the DVD an example is given of visualizing a brand-new car. You are to see yourself already seated in the car, enjoying the ride, thrilling to the experience. It is this power of visualizing that results in the car materializing.

How does this happen? It is not our job to worry about how it happens; it is our job to turn our desires over to the universe, for 'The hows are the domain of the universe; it always knows the shortest, quickest, fastest, most harmonious way between you and your dream.' 'If you turn it over to the universe you will be surprised and dazzled by what is delivered to you. This is where magic and miracles happen.' It is at this point in *The Secret* that we find the impersonal universe taking on personal (and Godlike) qualities: 'The universe knows; it delivers; it produces magic and miracles. It is for us to ask, believe, receive and visualize; it is for the universe to bring our desires to us.'

But beware! If you see and visualize negative things you will receive them as well. As a matter of fact, you must be careful not even to use negative words such as 'don't', 'no', or 'not'. For example, 'If you are thinking debt, even if you are thinking of getting out of debt, you are attracting debt.' Byrne goes so far as to state, 'Imperfect thoughts are the cause of all humanity's ills, including disease, poverty, and unhappiness.' Indeed, 'Anything we focus on we do create, so if we are really angry at a war that is going on or strife or suffering, we are adding energy to it ... and all of that only adds resistance.' Therefore, the anti-war movements create more war. The anti-drug movement creates more drugs, because we are focusing on what we don't want.

In addition, Byrne advises that we should shun those who are in these conditions so that we are not infected by their negative thoughts.

The spiritual teachings of *The Secret*

While *The Secret* lays little claim to be a religion, it certainly has religious overtones. In fact *The Secret* is clearly pantheistic, as is evident from the following quotes:

> Everything in the universe is energy [and] everything in the universe is connected; it is just one energy field, and energy is God; it is the same description, just different terminology.

> [Our physical being] just holds our spirit, and your spirit is so big, it fills the room; you are eternal life; you're source energy; you are God manifested in human form, made to perfection.

> Scripturally, we could say that we are the image and likeness of God. We could say that we are another way the universe is becoming conscious of itself.

Note the equation: everything in the universe is energy; energy is God; you are God; you are the universe. This is pure pantheism ('God is everything') and monism ('everything is one'). Such theology fits in well with Eastern religions (such as Buddhism and Hinduism) and its Western counterpart in what has historically been called the New Age movement. But this view of God and the universe is not Christian and certainly not biblical.

Drawing straight from its pantheistic roots, *The Secret* ascribes to people the very attributes of God. While Scripture tells us that God is the Creator, *The Secret* says that we have equal voice: 'You have God potential and power to create your world, and you are.' 'We are creators of our universe, and every wish of what we want to create will pass into our lives.'

And we are omnipotent:

> You are the designer of your destiny; you are the author; you write the story; the pen is in your hands, and the outcome is whatever you choose... Are there any limits to this? Absolutely not; we are unlimited beings; we have no ceiling; the capabilities and the talents and the gifts, the power which is in every single individual on this planet, is unlimited.

One contributor to the DVD even makes the obscure claim that 'You have enough power in your body to illuminate a whole city for nearly a week.'

Additionally we are our own final judge: 'Your purpose is what you say it is; your mission is the mission you give yourself; your life will be what you create it as and no one will stand in judgment, now or ever.'

The attributes that God claims for himself in Scripture are ascribed to humans in *The Secret*; therefore the true God is unneeded and unwanted in the system. Who needs a God when we are God? Who needs an all-powerful, all-wise, righteous, creator God when we, through the law of attraction, have all power, can tap into an all-wise universe to create our own world and no one can stand in judgment on what we do?

The Secret's links with other religions

While *The Secret* is clearly antithetical to biblical Christianity, it has many features in common with other religions. Below are some quick references.

Paganism

A number of years ago many people talked about the New Age movement. You don't hear much about this today because the

New Age movement has become mainstream; that is, its ideas have infiltrated our society. The New Age movement was basically paganism being introduced into the Western world. It was a belief in the spiritual world in the way that pagans have always believed. Today we hear that the Western world is 'more spiritual' than at any time in recent memory, but this spirituality is largely a pagan understanding of the spirit world.

We can see what paganism is by looking at its raw form as it exists in much of the world today. An excellent example is to be found in African traditional religions. African evangelical scholar Yusufu Turaki informs us that:

1. African religions are pragmatic. People want a religion that they can use to meet their needs and provide for their wishes.[16]

2. African religions are not cognitively oriented systems with esoteric doctrines and strict rules or regulations. Rather they are existential and experiential — more felt than understood.[17]

3. There are five fundamental beliefs of African religions.[18] These involve the existence of:

- Impersonal mystical powers[19]
- Spirit beings[20]
- Many divinities (this is why Africans can believe in Jesus without rejecting their other gods)
- A Supreme Being
- A hierarchy of spiritual beings and powers

4. Africans desire a religion of power.[21]

5. Even when Africans do become Christians, there is a tendency for Christianity to be seen as only a first step to greater mysteries and power.[22]

6. In African religions God is manipulated; in Christianity he is praised.[23]

7. Africans believe that words have innate power.[24]

8. Africans use magic to manipulate the world and spirits around them.[25]

From this brief outline of modern-day pagan beliefs it is easy to recognize that *The Secret* and paganism have many overlapping features.

Hinduism

The law of attraction has similar beliefs to those of Hinduism, especially as related to karma. Karma teaches that we ultimately receive what we deserve, what we attract — whether good or bad. When awful or great things happen, according to karma, they happen because our past actions warrant them. We ultimately get exactly what we deserve, or attract.

While karma is more concerned with morality than *The Secret* is, eventually we all attract exactly what we deserve although it may take many lifetimes (reincarnations). With the law of attraction we attract not so much what we deserve as what we want (*The Secret* has virtually nothing to do with right and wrong) and we do so in our lifetime. It turns out to be a handy system for Westerners who want everything yesterday and yet are enamoured with Eastern thought and practice.

Wicca

Like *The Secret*, Wicca sees God as an impersonal force. Wicca is an animistic religion which teaches that everything is imbued with a life force or energy. To practitioners of Wicca magic is essentially the idea that forces or spirits can be manipulated to accomplish personal objectives. Magic is 'the art or science of causing change to occur in conformity with will'.[26] The similarity to *The Secret* is obvious.

Many believe that adherents to Wicca are Satan-worshippers, but such is not the case. They actually deny the reality of Satan for much the same reason that *The Secret* spurns the negative. Wicca practitioners state, 'We believe that to give evil a name is to give evil power.'[27]

Gnosticism

Ancient Gnosticism, as well as its modern counterpart, Neo-Gnosticism, thrives on secrets and mysteries. Gnosticism was a counterfeit version of Christianity, beginning in the second century, which was full of esoteric secrets available only to an elite group of leaders who were in the know. *The Secret* fosters just such an atmosphere, complete with secrets known only to a few. These few, however, are willing to share what they know — for a price.

The Secret's Links with Christianity

New Thought

In my research for this chapter I was surprised to find that we have been down this road in the past. As a matter of fact, virtually the whole 'secret' was revealed in the mid-1800s, beginning with Phineas Quimby, who taught that:

> Physical diseases are caused by wrong thinking or false beliefs. Disease is merely an 'error' created 'not by God, but by man'. Eliminate false beliefs, Quimby taught, and the chief culprit for disease is thereby removed, yielding a healthy body.[28]

The New Thought movement developed from Quimby's ideas in the late 1860s:

> According to New Thought, human beings can experience health, success, and abundant life by using their thoughts to define the conditions of their lives. New Thought proponents subscribed to the 'law of attraction' [the same law behind

The Secret] which is the idea that our thoughts attract the things they want or expect.[29]

In New Thought, God is a universal force. God is pantheistic and man is viewed as divine; therefore man has unlimited potential.[30] And death is non-existent, being an entry into the fourth dimension of life.

Three major religious movements were spawned from New Thought: Christian Science, the United Church of Religious Science and the Unity School of Christianity. These are collectively known as the 'mind sciences'.[31]

We know therefore from history what the law of attraction attracts: it attracts false religious systems, systems Paul called 'doctrines of demons' (1 Tim. 4:1).

The Word of Faith Movement

The Secret teaches that we can 'create [our] own happiness through the law of attraction'. Whether it is cash, health, prosperity or happiness that we desire, all can be ours if we will just learn to use *The Secret*. We are told, 'Disease cannot live in a body that is in a healthy emotional state.' But be warned: 'If you have a disease and you are focusing on it and talking to people about it, you are going to create more disease cells.'

Such rhetoric should sound familiar to anyone who is even faintly aware of the Word of Faith Movement, often termed, 'the prosperity gospel'. This group has been infiltrating biblical Christianity for years and is now the fastest-growing segment of Christianity in the world. Some have estimated that up to 90% of those claiming to be Christians in Africa are of the prosperity-gospel variety. I will deal more with the prosperity gospel in the next chapter, but for now let's turn to a biblical response to these false teachings.

A biblical response

Satan loves to take truth and lace it with poison (2 Cor. 11:3,14,15). For this reason we are never afforded the luxury of being naïve. We must always be careful that we are not deceived by the empty imitations and lies that are in our world system (Col. 2:8).

More to the point, God condemns all forms of divination, witchcraft and sorcery, which are attempts to manipulate the spirit world, including God himself (Lev. 19:31; Deut. 18:9-14; 1 Sam. 28:3,9; 2 Kings 23:24; Isa. 8:19-20; Acts 19:18-19; Jer. 27:8-9). *The Secret* definitely falls under this prohibition as it seeks to teach methods of controlling the universe which are forbidden by God.

Even those who have missed the sorcery connection found in *The Secret* should not fail to miss the selfishness and greed factors, since Scripture so clearly condemns both (Matt. 6:19; 1 Tim. 6:7-10; Heb. 13:5). In watching the DVD one is clearly struck with the self-centredness and avarice of *The Secret*. At no point does anyone visualize helping the poor or sick or needy. The things to be attracted are personal health, wealth and happiness. In *The Secret* 'You' are at the centre of the universe, even the universe itself. More to the point — you are God. Just in case anyone missed this, read carefully the words of Rhonda Byrne:

> You are God in a physical body. You are Spirit in flesh. You are Eternal Life expressing itself as You. You are a cosmic being. You are all power. You are all wisdom. You are all intelligence. You are perfection. You are magnificence. You are creator, and you are creating the creation of You on this planet.[32]

Byrne concludes her book with this statement:

> The earth turns on its orbit for You. The oceans ebb and flow for You. The birds sing for You. The sun rises and it sets for You. The stars come out for You. Every beautiful thing you see, every wondrous thing you experience, is all there for

You. Take a look around. None of it can exist, without You. No matter who you thought you were, now you know the Truth of Who You Really Are. You are the master of the Universe. You are the heir to the kingdom. You are the perfection of Life. And now you know The Secret.[33]

Still, some might ask, what harm is done? One critic of *The Secret* has suggested the following:

The danger to society is not merely that it should believe wrong things, though that is great enough, but that it should become credulous, and lose the habit of testing things and inquiring into them, for then it must sink back into savagery... It may matter little to me, in my cloud-castle of sweet illusions and darling lies; but it matters much to Man that I have made my neighbors ready to deceive. The credulous man is father to the liar and the cheat.[34]

Even more importantly, the teachings of *The Secret* are unbiblical. To live in the sphere of such lies is to live falsely and, despite *The Secret's* disclaimer, there is a Judge of this universe, and what we do and how we live matters to him.

The purpose of life is to glorify God, not self. The great problem of mankind is sin, not negative thinking. With Isaiah we must cry:

When they say to you, 'Consult the mediums and the spiritists who whisper and mutter,' should not a people consult their God?... To the law and to the testimony! If they do not speak according to this word, it is because they have no dawn (Isa. 8:19-20).

4

The Prosperity Gospel
Goes Mainstream

As we saw in the last chapter, paganism has become extremely winsome to many today as a result of the infiltration of such materials as *The Secret*, which claims that we can create our own happiness through the law of attraction. Whatever we desire can be ours if only we learn to use 'the secret'. While some of the terms may differ, the concepts behind *The Secret*, and similar 'new spirituality' and Eastern teachings, have been making the rounds throughout various segments of Christianity for years. Often called the 'Word of Faith' movement, or simply the 'Faith' movement by its friends, and 'the prosperity gospel', or 'name-it-and-claim it' by sceptics, it has become a powerful force throughout the world. 17% of Christians, according to a poll conducted in 2006, consider themselves to be part of the movement.[1]

Well-known personalities within the movement include Kenneth Hagin (deceased), Kenneth Copeland, Robert Tilton, Paul Yonggi Cho, Benny Hinn, Marilyn Hickey, Frederick Price, John Avanzini, Charles Capps, Jerry Savelle, Morris Cerullo, Joyce Meyer and Paul and Jan Crouch.

As implied by the title 'Word of Faith', the supporters of this movement believe that faith works like a mighty power, or force. Through faith we can obtain anything we want — health, wealth, success, or whatever we please. However, this force is released only through the *spoken word*. As we speak words of faith, power is discharged to achieve our desires.

In *Christianity in Crisis*, Hank Hanegraaff summarizes the theology of Kenneth Hagin (considered by many to be the father of this movement) as found in his booklet *How to Write Your Own Ticket with God*:

> In the opening chapter, titled 'Jesus Appears to Me', Hagin claims that while he was 'in the Spirit', Jesus told him to get a pencil and a piece of paper. He then instructed him to 'write down: 1, 2, 3, 4'. Jesus then allegedly told Hagin that 'if anybody, anywhere, will take these four steps or put these four principles into operation, he will always receive whatever he wants from Me or from God the Father'. That includes whatever you want financially. The formula is simply: 'Say it, Do it, Receive it, and Tell it.'
>
> 1. Step number one is 'Say it.' 'Positive or negative, it is up to the individual. According to what the individual says, that shall he receive.'
> 2. Step number two is 'Do it.' 'Your action defeats you or puts you over. According to your action, you receive or you are kept from receiving.'
> 3. Step number three is 'Receive it.' We are to plug into the 'powerhouse of heaven'. *'Faith is the plug*, praise God! Just plug in.'
> 4. Step number four is 'Tell it so others may believe.' This final step might be considered the Faith movement's outreach program.[2]

Kenneth Copeland states the faith formula this way: 'All it takes is 1) seeing or visualizing whatever you need, whether physical or financial; 2) staking your claim on Scripture; and 3) speaking it into existence.'[3]

Paul Yonggi Cho, pastor of the world's largest church in South Korea, borrowing from the occult, has developed what he calls the 'Law of Incubation'. Here is how it works: 'First make a clear-cut goal, then draw a mental picture, vivid and graphic, to visualize success. Then incubate it into reality, and finally speak it into existence through the creative power of the spoken word.'⁴

If a positive confession of faith releases good things, a negative confession can actually backfire. Capps says the tongue 'can kill you, or it can release the life of God within you'. This is so because 'Faith is a seed ... you plant it by speaking it.' There is power in 'the evil fourth dimension', says Cho.

Hagin explains that if you confess sickness you get sickness; if you confess health you get health; whatever you say, you get. The commonly held view of the movement is that the spoken word releases power — power for good or power for evil. It is easy to see why the title 'positive confession' is another title that is often applied to this group.

As you might guess, the teachings of the Word of Faith movement are very attractive to some. If we can create whatever our hearts desire by simply demanding what we want by faith, if we can manipulate the universe, and perhaps even God, then we have our own personal genie just waiting to fulfil our wishes. The similarities between Word of Faith teachings and *The Secret* are unmistakable.

The new look: Joel Osteen

Many Christians can discern the obvious error of New Age teachings behind *The Secret* and similar books such as Eckhart Tolle's *The New Earth*, as well as the over-the-top proclamations of many within the prosperity-gospel movement. However, when similar teachings are repackaged, reworded and presented in a winsome fashion, a larger number will fall prey. Enter Joel Osteen and his brand of the prosperity 'gospel'. As Michael Horton has noted, 'Osteen has achieved the dubious success of making the "name-it-claim-it" philosophy of Kenneth Copeland and Benny Hinn mainstream.'⁵ As we shall see, Osteen teaches essentially the same theology as his Word of Faith mentors, but he gives it an updated twist.

Joel Osteen has become a household name as a result of his incredible success. He 'pastors' the largest church in America, Lakewood Church in Houston, Texas, which in 2008 boasted an average weekend attendance of 43,500, almost double that of its nearest competitor.[6] Osteen took the helm of Lakewood Church in 1999 upon the death of his father, John. John Osteen was openly a prosperity-gospel preacher who founded Lakewood in 1959 and had built it into a 6,000-member church before his son replaced him. Joel, who until that point had given leadership to the television ministry of Lakewood and had preached only once before, was thrust into the pulpit and immediately the church began to explode. Today Lakewood services are broadcast in over 100 countries; Joel has written two multi-million-seller books, and he, along with his wife, mother and numerous musicians from Lakewood, travels throughout the world offering an event they call 'A Night of Hope'. While most churches struggle to find and keep members, people are willing to purchase $15 tickets to attend 'A Night of Hope' and the auditoriums are usually packed.

Osteen has no theological training and it is obvious from his books, sermons and interviews on television that he has little knowledge of the Scriptures. Nevertheless, he has caught an unprecedented wave of popularity and could clearly claim the title of the most admired pastor in America. This popularity is, of course, due largely to his message. Eschewing anything controversial or negative (such as hell, or judgment, or even sin), Osteen proclaims a message of pure positivism. The title of his first book, *Your Best Life Now,* summarizes what Osteen has to offer his many audiences. If we will follow certain principles, or steps (seven to be exact), so the storyline goes, our existence will be happy, healthy and blessed with everything that would make this life wonderful. This is a message that appeals to the flesh of unbelievers and worldly-minded Christians and would account for the superstar status that Osteen now has.

Of course this is a harsh accusation. I am charging Joel Osteen with being a false teacher — a man who has twisted the gospel to entice the fallen nature of people, who has turned God into a genie and who has distorted Scripture to present a warm and fuzzy yet warped form of Christianity. In order to see if I am correct, or just being mean-spirited, we need to turn to Osteen's actual words as found in *Your Best Life Now*.

What the reader will find in this best-selling book is a mixture of common sense, helpful practical advice and a multitude of success stories interlaced with a heavy dose of deceitful teaching. Let's begin with the gospel. It is not so much that Osteen presents a false gospel (which he seems to do in *Your Best Life Now*), but rather, no gospel at all. In a 300-page book which will be read by millions of unbelievers, the closest Osteen ever comes to the gospel is: 'Work out your own salvation. Salvation is more than a onetime prayer. It is constantly working with God, dealing with the issues He brings up and keeping a good attitude, fighting through until you win the victory.'[7] What Osteen believes concerning the gospel is uncertain, but what is undeniable is that the emphasis of his ministry is maintaining a positive outlook on life rather than a right relationship with God. Except for this one sentence, the entirely of the book is taken up with 'seven steps to living at your full potential', as stated in the subtitle. This theme resonates with the thinking of those whose lives and minds are in conformity with this world system rather than being 'transformed by the renewing of [their minds]' (Rom. 12:2).

It really should not surprise us that men like Osteen have caught the public's eye — they tell us what we, by nature, already believe (2 Tim. 4:3), which is that we need to make the best of this life and enjoy every minute we can, because this is the best it is ever going to be. This philosophy is the world's, not God's, who consistently calls us to live for higher values than this world and self (1 John 2:15-17). As Paul wrote to the church at Colossae, 'Set your mind on the things above, not on the things that are on earth' (Col. 3:2). Paul did not mean by this that we are to ignore life on this planet and go and hide somewhere until the Lord returns, as conservative Christians are often accused of doing. It means that we live for a higher purpose than personal pleasure and success, 'for you have died and your life is hidden with Christ in God' (Col. 3:3). Osteen makes no attempt to draw his readers to this higher purpose, to a life lived for God. Instead God is to be manipulated for our own pleasure. I think Osteen would appreciate Eliphaz's advice to Job (later condemned by God): 'Yield now and be at peace with Him; thereby good will come to you' (Job 22:21).

Let's take a look at some specifics of Osteen's message.

The offer

Osteen's attraction is found in what he is offering, which is nothing less than a life of good health, abundance, wealth, prosperity and success: 'If you develop an image of victory, success, health, abundance, joy, peace, and happiness, nothing on earth will be able to hold those things from you.'[8] Since these are the things most people treasure, and since Jesus informed us that 'where your treasure is, there your heart will be also' (Matt. 6:21), it is predictable that the seductive promise of a map leading to these treasures would find many adherents. And it certainly does. But what specifically is being offered?

Health

If we follow the teachings of Osteen we can expect good health. His mother, for example, was diagnosed with terminal cancer twenty years ago, but because she confessed good health she is cancer-free today.[9] As a matter of fact, one of the highlights of the 'Night of Hope' events is the testimony by Osteen's mother concerning her physical healing — implying of course, that those in the audience can also be healed if only they will do what Joel suggests.

Abundance

Osteen declares, without qualification, that all of us are destined for greatness of every kind — and abundance: 'You were born to win; you were born for greatness, you were created to be a champion in life.'[10] 'He wants you to live in abundance. He wants to give you the desires of your heart... God is turning things around in your favor.'[11] In fact, apparently irrespective of our relationship with God, 'Before we were ever formed, He programmed us to live abundant lives, to be happy, healthy, and whole. But when our thinking becomes contaminated it is no longer in line with God's Word.'[12]

Two things should be noted at this juncture.

First, *the Scriptures teach no such thing.* While eternal life with the Lord is the ultimate destiny of the redeemed, judgment and then the lake of fire is the ultimate destiny of the lost (2 Thess. 1:9; Rev. 20:14-15). In the meantime, in this life the rain falls on the just and the unjust, and Christians may suffer as many trials as unbelievers, perhaps more (Rom. 5:3-5; James 1:2-4; 2 Cor. 4:8-12; 11:23-29; Heb 11:35-40). It is true that Psalm 37:4 promises, 'Delight yourself in the LORD; and He will give you the desires of your heart,' but upon a little reflection it will be seen that one who delights himself in the Lord desires God, not mere material blessings, good parking spots, success in business and a fine wardrobe. Osteen's program trivializes the abundant life Jesus came to give his followers (John 10:10).

Secondly, when the prosperity teachers use the phrase 'God's Word', the reader must carefully discern what is meant. Often, as in this case, *'God's Word' is not a reference to the Bible*, but to words spoken, supposedly by God, extra-biblically through the Word of Faith adherents. Osteen, then, is not accusing people of being out of step with the Scriptures, but of being out of step with the teachings of men such as himself. This is nothing less than a claim that God has revealed his Word apart from Scripture and through prosperity leaders.

Wealth

'God wants to increase you financially, by giving you promotions, fresh ideas and creativity',[13] or so Osteen promises. How does he know this — since in biblical times promotions were not common practice, fresh ideas and creativity did not carry the value they do today and wealth was not necessarily seen as a sign of God's pleasure? Someone might counter that David and Solomon were wealthy, but this was not the case for Jeremiah and Habakkuk, both godly men who lost everything. Job flourished for a time, lost it all and then gained it back. Did one of Job's 'comforters' clue him in on prosperity philosophy in order for him to regain his wealth? Was that the turning point? Hardly. It was when Job repented of his arrogance that God restored his former affluence, and God was under no obligation to do that. The scriptural principle is that the Lord is sovereignly at work in our lives. He can choose to bless us with riches, or he can choose to bless us by taking our riches away. This is not to negate the place of hard work and a proper attitude on our part, but it does recognize the sovereign role that God plays in every aspect of our lives. And the bottom line is that the Lord never promises us wealth in this life.

So where does Osteen come up with the idea that 'God wants to increase us financially'? His basis is in his very limited and selective experience. He tells us, for example, that when his father was 'willing to go beyond the barriers of the past' by applying the principles found in Joel's book, '… he broke that curse of poverty in our family. Now, my siblings and I, and our children, grandchildren, even great-grandchildren, are all going to experience more of the goodness [i.e. wealth] of God because of what one man did.'[14]

Of course, millions of examples throughout the world and throughout history could be given of godly people living in poverty, and of the children of the wealthy wasting their inheritance and privileges, but Osteen seems to conveniently ignore such examples. Instead he is convinced that 'God wants to give you your own house.'[15] The US government and the banking system seemed to agree with Osteen until the recent economic crash. Now they are taking away many of those houses. But this does not deter Osteen; he is persuaded that we will prosper.

Prosperity

Prosperity is more than health and wealth; it includes all the good things life can give. Apparently God is working extra hard to make life easy for us. Osteen promises, 'It's going to happen... Suddenly, your situation will change for the better... He will bring your dreams to pass.'[16]

Such statements leave no room for the cancer patient who does not get better, the factory worker who is laid off and never again finds a comparable job, the athlete who has a career-ending injury, or all those losers at the 'American Idol', or 'Britain's Got Talent' auditions (we can be thankful for this one at least!). Such people would have reason to question Osteen's pronouncement that 'God didn't make you to be average. God created you to excel.'[17] Just two minutes of reflection would unveil the fallacy of this statement By definition everyone cannot be above average — somebody has to be in the middle of the pack, and someone has to bring up the rear. This kind of idea sounds like the familiar grade inflation going on in many of our schools and universities today. If 90% of students all make an 'A' average (which is not uncommon any more) that does not mean that they are brighter than past students; it just means that the evaluation system has been changed so that more students (and potential employers) think they are successful.

In addition, didn't Paul tell us that, of the ones God calls, there are 'not many wise ..., not many mighty, not many noble; but God has chosen the foolish things of the world to shame the wise...'? (1 Cor. 1:27). Our Lord seems to have standards and values that are out of alignment with Osteen's.

Still Osteen insists: 'You will often receive preferential treatment simply because your Father is the King of kings, and His glory and honor spill over onto you.'[18] Osteen prays, 'Father, I thank you that I have Your favor.'[19] By God's favour Osteen has in mind such earth-shaking issues as finding the perfect parking spot in a crowded lot.[20] Why a perfectly healthy middle-aged man would pray for the prime parking spot, knowing of course that someone with greater physical needs may be denied such a spot, is never explained. Osteen admits that God sometimes refuses to answer his prayer about parking, but this 'doesn't mean that I am going to quit believing in the favor of God'.[21] Osteen can't lose. If he finds the best spot in the lot he has God's favour; if he has to drive around for fifteen minutes and fails in this all-important task, he is not going to let it derail his theology.

Success

'God wants you to go further than your parents.'[22] This statement is made without a speck of biblical evidence. On the contrary, it was a rarity in Scripture to find a child who exceeded a godly or successful parent. Further, the same is often true in our own experience — some children go further than their parents; others do not. Osteen is making an unsupportable statement.

But, not to be deterred, we are told: 'God wants you to live an overcoming life of victory. He doesn't want you to barely get by. He's called *El Shaddai*, "the God of more than enough".'[23] On the contrary, *El Shaddai* is a title used for our Lord in the Old Testament which is often translated 'God Almighty'. It speaks of the all-sufficiency of God, and is a special title of reverence. Osteen has invented his own meaning and in the process turned God into our personal sugar daddy, ready to hand out the goodies to any who think they have discovered the secret way to his heart.

Good self-image

'God wants us to have healthy, positive self-images, to see ourselves as priceless treasures. He wants us to feel good about ourselves... God sees you as a champion... He regards you as a strong, courageous, successful, overcoming person.'[24] Really? From what source does Osteen draw his view of self-image? Certainly not from Scripture, which never mentions such a thing.

Rather than chase after good self-images, Paul warns us 'not to think more highly of [ourselves] than [we] ought to think; but to think so as to have sound judgment' (Rom. 12:3). But instead of taking seriously the instruction of Scripture, Osteen is happy to chase after the fads found in pop-psychology. He goes on: 'When you are tempted to get discouraged, remind yourself that according to God's Word, your future is getting brighter; you are on your way to a new level of glory.'[25] Eternally this is a true statement for the child of God, but to promise that such will be the case in this life (and keep in mind that Osteen is concerned with this life now) is pure deception. And since Osteen makes no distinction between the redeemed and the unregenerate in his book, he is offering a false and damning hope to most of his audience — those who do not know Christ as their Saviour.

The belief system

Upon what does Osteen base his belief system? It is certainly not Scripture, for the Bible never teaches anything remotely similar to this prosperity brand of Christianity. That is not to say that *Your Best Life Now* is totally devoid of biblical references, but the few that are attempted are almost all hopelessly out of context or twisted beyond recognition.[26] Osteen gives notice early and often that his views are not drawn fundamentally from Scripture but from his experiences and those of others. Still, in the introduction he writes:

> Within these pages, you will find seven simple, yet profound, steps to improve your life, regardless of your current level of success or lack of it. I know these steps work, because they have worked in the lives of my family members, friends, and associates, as well as in my own life.[27]

Osteen supports his thesis through the use of numerous success stories of one type or another. Some of his stories are impossible, and/or at best incapable of being documented and therefore raise a red flag concerning his integrity.[28] Others are highly selective examples of happy endings.[29]

As a result of such stories Osteen can promise that, if his theories are embraced, 'suddenly, things will change, suddenly, that business will take off. Suddenly, your husband will desire a relationship with God. Suddenly, that wayward child will come home. Suddenly, God will bring your hopes and dreams to pass.'[30] Or maybe not! Inexplicably (given his belief system and insistence that God will bring prosperity to our lives if we follow the formula), Osteen has to admit that all things do not end in success. Both his sister and father experienced the failure of divorce;[31] some people are not healed;[32] things don't always work out the way we desire;[33] his father suffered kidney failure and was on dialysis for years[34] and died of a heart attack.[35] While Osteen declares, 'God does not send problems', he admits that 'sometimes He allows us to go through them'.[36] But the fact is that, even in Osteen's story-theology world, the people of God suffer the same ups and downs, successes and failures, health and sickness, and so forth, as the unbeliever. One has only to glance through the psalms to realize that this is not our 'best life now'. We live in a corrupt world and until the Lord returns our sin-tainted universe will often disappoint and grieve us. Stories of success (and failure) can be lined up from here to eternity, but such stories are not the basis of truth, or of life; the Word of God is.

The methods

Drawing, however, from many selective stories, and ignoring what God has to say, Osteen presents a methodology that he promises will produce a life of abundance, success, health and affluence. This system is not unique to Osteen, having come almost verbatim from the prosperity teachers mentioned above, but he has taken this false teaching to a new audience. Let's examine how the program works.

There are three basic steps to 'your best life now'.

Visualization

The initial step in Osteen's program is visualization:

> The first step to living at your full potential is to *enlarge your vision*. To live your best life now, you must start looking at life through eyes of faith, seeing yourself rising to new levels. See your business taking off. See your marriage restored. See your family prospering. See your dreams coming to pass. You must conceive it and believe it is possible if you ever hope to experience it [emphasis his].[37]

The reason why visualization is necessary is because it has the power to bring about what you envisage:

> You will produce what you're continually seeing in your mind... If you develop an image of victory, success, health, abundance, joy, peace, and happiness, nothing on earth will be able to hold those things from you... Start anticipating promotions and supernatural increase. You must conceive it in your heart and mind before you can receive it... You must make room for increase in your own thinking, and then God will bring those things to pass.[38]

Apparently even God is at the mercy of that which we visualize; after all, 'Thoughts [not God?] determine destiny.'[39] 'If you don't think your body can be healed, it never will be... When you think positive, excellent thoughts, you will be propelled toward greatness, inevitably bound for increase, promotion, and God's supernatural blessings.'[40]

Faith

It is not enough to think about and visualize what we want; we must also express faith: 'God works by faith. You must believe first, and then you'll receive.'[41] 'We receive what we believe. Unfortunately, this principle works as strongly in the negative as it does in the positive.'[42] 'Understand this: God will help you, but you cast the deciding vote ... [we must] get into agreement with God.'[43] 'It's our faith that activates the power of God.'[44]

It is vital that we visualize what we want and that we expect it because our faith attracts what we visualize. While Osteen never calls this the 'law of attraction', notice its similarity to the same concept as taught by New Age teachers such as Eckhart Tolle, Rhonda Byrne and others: 'Your life will follow your expectations. What you expect is what you will get.'[45]

> Our thoughts contain tremendous power. Remember, we draw into our lives that which we constantly think about. If we're always dwelling on the negative, we will attract negative people, experiences, and attitudes. If we're always dwelling on our fears, we will draw in more fear. You are setting the direction of your life with your thoughts.[46]

Words

Still, it is not enough to think good thoughts and express faith in them; it is necessary to speak your desires out loud. This is why the prosperity gospel is often called the 'Word of Faith' movement — for power lies in the spoken word. Follow Osteen's thinking:

> Our words have tremendous power, and whether we want to or not, we will give life to what we're saying, either good or bad... Words are similar to seeds, by speaking them aloud, they are planted in our subconscious minds, and they take on a life of their own.[47]

Osteen suggests:

> Get up each morning and look in the mirror and say, 'I am valuable. I am loved. God has a great plan for my life. I have favor wherever I go. God's blessings are chasing me down and overtaking me. Everything I touch prospers and succeeds. I'm excited about my future!' Start speaking those

kinds of words, and before long, you will rise to a new level of well-being, success, and victory. There truly is power in your words.[48]

But there is more. We must also speak to our problems:

Whatever your mountain is, you must do more than think about it, more than pray about it; you must speak to that obstacle... Start calling yourself healed, happy, whole, blessed, and prosperous. Stop talking to God about how big your mountains are, and start talking to your mountains about how big your God is.[49]

Osteen can confidently promise us, 'Friend, there is a miracle in your mouth.'[50] How so? 'The moment you speak something out, you give birth to it. This is a spiritual principle, and it works whether what you are saying is good or bad, positive or negative.'[51] Therefore, 'You must start boldly confessing God's Word, using your words to move forward in life, to bring to life the great things God has in store for you.'[52]

And it is totally up to us to pull off this kind of life:

God has already done everything He's going to do. The ball is now in your court. If you want success, if you want wisdom, if you want to be prosperous and healthy, you're going to have to do more than meditate and believe; you must boldly declare words of faith and victory over yourself and your family.[53]

Osteen is presenting a pure self-help program and baptizing it in the name of God. Those who fail to reach these promised benefits have only themselves to blame, since they apparently did not follow Osteen's formula.

Conclusion

Whenever the supposed things of God and people of God become popular with the inhabitants of this fallen world, we would be wise to walk softly and be extra discerning. The Jews persecuted and/or killed almost every one of their prophets (Acts 7:52); the apostles were despised by the world, and Jesus was murdered by those he came to save. Jesus pronounced a blessing on those who are persecuted for the sake of righteousness (Matt. 5:11) and warned, 'If they persecuted Me, they will also persecute you' (John 15:20). Why? Because the message of the cross 'is foolishness to those who are perishing' (1 Cor. 1:18). Therefore when we find a Christian message or ministry or man or woman being praised by unbelievers, we can be assured that either unregenerate humanity has not yet caught on to what is being said, or else that the message that is being proclaimed is in line with the worldview of the unbeliever. As has been demonstrated, Osteen's message is exactly what unbelievers and undiscerning Christians want to believe and they are thrilled to have someone who claims to be a reliable spokesperson for God who agrees with them. This would account for Osteen's incredible success, but it does not account for, or excuse, the inconceivable gullibility and immaturity of professing Christians.

5

The Challenge of Pragmatism

If there is a common religion to be found within the Western world it surely is pragmatism — the religion of 'What works?' Pragmatism has no cathedrals; it follows no liturgy, hires no pastors and cannot be found in any listing of denominations, yet it is woven into the very fabric of the Western church. Whether we are talking about mainline, Pentecostal, fundamentalist, emergent or orthodox, it does not take much observation to realize that pragmatism is a strand that runs throughout each tradition. To attempt to remove pragmatism is to pull a thread which could very well unravel the whole structure of Christianity and church life as we know it today, yet pull on that thread we must. The problem is that far too many of us are willing to use any approach available to accomplish our goals, even if those approaches and/or goals do not mesh with the revealed will of God. Our creed is: 'If it works it must be of God,' for, after all, the outward blessing of God is the criterion by which we often measure the approval of God. By using the standard of pragmatism rather than Scripture, we can with all good conscience live lives and develop ministries that have the appearance of wisdom but nevertheless fall seriously short of God's standard. We would do well to ponder the warning found in Proverbs 14:12: 'There is a way which seems right to a man, but its end is the way of death.'

Take, for example, the wildly popular and thoroughly pragmatic book *Blue Like Jazz* by Donald Miller. The cover of *Blue Like Jazz* tells us that it was written for 'anyone wondering if the Christian faith is still relevant in a post-modern culture' and 'for anyone thirsting for a fresh encounter with a God who is real'. Yet Miller uses not a single biblical quote or reference and only in passing mentions scriptural situations as he purports to lead us towards an authentic encounter with God. It is for this reason that he can sing the praises of one of the most depraved college campuses in the world (by Miller's own admission) while telling us, 'I had more significant spiritual experiences at Reed College than I ever had at church.'[1]

Miller would have us disregard the guidance of Psalm 1:1, 'How blessed is the man who does not walk in the counsel of the wicked, nor stand in the path of sinners, nor sit in the seat of scoffers!' and replace it with his own counsel because this is his 'experience'. For example, Miller tells us that he can partially agree with what Christians are saying about depravity (a teaching derived from the Bible, by the way), not because it is biblical, but because of his 'experience' with his own depravity.[2] Moreover, Miller speaks of a time when he was living with 'hippies' who 'smoked a lot of pot [and] drank a lot of beer,' were apparently immoral and stole food, yet, he says, 'I pull them [the hippies] out when I need to be reminded about goodness, about purity and kindness.'[3]

It is not Scripture which guides Miller's thoughts, but situations that seem to work for him and appear to be in agreement with his own experience. Pragmatism rules in Miller's book and resonates with millions of his readers. The Christian community has grown so used to this type of thinking that few flinch when Christian leaders, like Miller, build a whole scheme of living around what seems to be working for them.

The philosophical foundation

While pragmatism is simply a way of life to most people, it is also a philosophical system. One Christian thinker reminds us that:

> [Philosopher Immanuel Kant (1724–1804)] made it intellectually fashionable both to doubt that we can know reality as it is and to focus on practical things, like ethics. Later that would be echoed in the pragmatism of John Dewey (1859–1952) and the neo-Pragmatism of Richard Rorty (1931–) [one of the originators of postmodern philosophy], who both suggest that we cannot know reality in any full and final sense; we must settle for what works.[4]

Few people have extensive understanding of philosophy, but it doesn't take a philosopher to recognize that the prevailing attitude today, an attitude which has invaded the church, is to 'settle for what works' and not be overly concerned about truth. After all, postmodernists believe that we can never be certain of truth anyway; therefore pragmatism will have to do. But when we exchange truth for what works — or, rather, what we think works — we have elevated our thoughts above God's. Or, as Gordon Clark warns, 'Since God is truth, a contempt for truth is equally a contempt for God.'[5]

Whatever is making the rounds in philosophical circles usually manages to find its way into Christian thinking as well. J. Gresham Machen said it well almost a century ago: 'What is today a matter of academic speculation begins tomorrow to move armies and pull down empires.'[6] One of the academic speculations which is popular at the moment is portraying modern evangelicalism as a product of the Enlightenment, with its emphasis on science, reason and systematic thought. This is especially true among those who embrace a postmodern form of Christianity, such as the emergent church leaders. For example, Robert Webber writes:

Conservatives followed the Enlightenment's emphasis on individualism, reason, and objective truth to build edifices of certainty drawing from the internal consistency of the Bible, the doctrine of inerrancy, the apologetic use of archaeology, critical defense of the biblical text, and other such attempts at rational proof... This Enlightenment paradigm produced three convictions shared equally by Christians and non-Christians: foundationalism, structuralism, and the notion of the metanarrative.[7]

By linking such things as inerrancy, apologetics, foundationalism, and so forth, with the Enlightenment, emerging Christian thinkers attempt to undermine these concepts in the eyes of the modern church. If these ideas spring from Enlightenment philosophy, then they can be discarded as worthless and we can march on to other philosophies, such as ones being proposed by postmodernism, or so the reasoning goes. The issue, however, is not whether something we have embraced happens to agree, or disagree, with a particular line of thinking, but whether what we believe agrees with Scripture. Certainly there are elements of truth in the accusations made by postmodern Christians. But it should be recalled that most evangelical leaders (both past and present) have made concerted attempts to filter out the deadly beliefs of the Enlightenment while retaining those parts which were helpful. For example, our final authority does not rest in reason and science (Enlightenment philosophy), but in Scripture (biblical teaching). Christians do not draw their thinking from the Enlightenment; nevertheless they maintain that Christianity is a reasonable faith, that the Bible is understandable and that truth can be analysed and systematized.

Still the criticism is valid that theology can be so standardized as to remove the wonder of God, leaving behind an outline of doctrines with no life pulsating in its veins. Countless believers can regurgitate their theological beliefs and favourite memorized Scripture verses, yet know virtually nothing of dynamic Christian living. Rote memory and sound doctrine are not equivalent to a passionate, heartfelt love for Christ — but neither are they extra baggage. Emergent thinkers and communicators provide a needed correction when they demonstrate that knowledge does not automatically lead to spiritual vitality, but they go too far when they say that spiritual vitality can be found apart from a solid understanding of the truth of God's revelation. This route has been travelled before, and not that long ago, with disastrous results.

From philosophy to theology

As a matter of fact, I believe that what we are seeing today in much of popular evangelicalism is not the residue of the Enlightenment but of Romanticism. Historian David Bebbington tells us that in the nineteenth century a new way of looking at the world (Romanticism) arose to challenge, and to some degree supplant, Enlightenment thinking. Bebbington observes:

> Instead of exalting reason [as the Enlightenment did], those touched by the new spirit of the times placed their emphasis on will, spirit and emotion. They wanted to escape the tight framework of thinking imposed by the older rational approach in order to breathe a freer air.[8]

Bebbington informs us that it was Horace Bushnell, around the midpoint of the nineteenth century, who popularized Romantic ideas so that they began to seep into the theology of evangelicalism. Bushnell would write, 'All formulas of doctrine should be held in a certain spirit of accommodation. They cannot be pressed to the letter for the very sufficient reason that the letter is never true.'[9] Bushnell argued that Christian truth should appeal to 'feeling and imaginative reason', not to 'the natural understanding'.[10]

If this kind of language sounds familiar it should do. Post-modernists, including those found within the church, would feel quite at home with Romanticism, since postmodern thinking is similar. It should therefore be carefully noted where Romanticism led evangelicals during the 1800s — straight to theological liberalism. During the latter part of the nineteenth century virtually all cardinal doctrines of the faith were challenged or denied by the growing liberalism (derived mostly from German Rationalism and Higher Criticism) which was threatening the evangelical church. From the Godhead to the necessity for salvation, to the existence of hell, to the atonement, to the inspiration of Scripture, to the very meaning of the gospel, every doctrine held precious by the evangelical community was gutted of biblical meaning and infused with ideas fitting the times.

Church historian and theologian Iain Murray documents the fact that Friedrich Schleiermacher (1768–1834), considered the father of theological liberalism, 'adopted the Romanticism of Rousseau and the pantheism of other contemporary philosophers ... [and] came forward to assert that religion is primarily not a matter of doctrine but rather of feeling, intuition and experience.'[11] 'Life, not theology' became the battle cry of the Romanticized, liberal church of the 1800s. As a result, matters of belief were considered of little consequence; what was important was life and experience. Orthopraxy (correct practice, or living) triumphed over orthodoxy (correct doctrine). This was an overreaction by a Christian community which had been softened up by the infiltration of Romanticism. True, biblical Christianity has always confirmed the necessity of both life *and* experience. No church leaders I know are content with developing people whose heads are full of knowledge but whose lives are full of sin. However, the contention of conservative believers has always been that life emerges from sound doctrine; right living is never formed in a truth vacuum. Joel Beeke had it right when he wrote, 'Doctrine must produce life, and life must adorn doctrine.'[12]

The mood of our current postmodern moment, however, like the Romantics and liberals of the 1800s, is to minimize doctrine to the point of its being non-essential and to maximize life and experience divorced from a theological core. Brian McLaren, a prominent leader in the emergent movement (the twenty-first century's version of old liberalism), writes, 'We place less emphasis on whose lineage, rites, doctrines, structures, and terminology are *right* and more emphasis on whose actions, service, outreach, kindness, and effectiveness are *good*' (emphasis his).[13] McLaren would not claim that all doctrines are wrong, but since we can never be certain which doctrines are correct, we must practise what he calls 'generous orthodoxy', which is little different from saying, 'Everyone is right and everyone is wrong, so let's just get along and love everybody.' McLaren seems unconcerned that it is virtually impossible to determine what is good unless one first knows what is right.

Emergent pastor Rob Bell concurs with McLaren's emphasis: 'Perhaps a better question than who's right, is who's living rightly?'[14] Bell then illustrates his convictions through the use of a trampoline. In Bell's illustration the springs that hold the tarpaulin to the frame are Christian doctrines, and even the most sacred doctrines (springs) are dispensable. He offers the doctrine of the incarnation as an example, suggesting that if it could be proved that Jesus was not born of a virgin it would not in any sense affect the Christian faith.[15] The big question for Bell is not what is true. Instead he wants to know, 'Is the way of Jesus still the best possible way to live?'[16] This pragmatic question is Bell's one essential for the Christian life. Bell is 'far more interested in jumping than … arguing about whose trampoline is better'.[17] In other words, what matters is how we live, not what we believe. These men see no vital connection between what we believe and how we live, between orthodoxy and orthopraxy. Having accepted this disconnect, they move on to elevate orthopraxy to the exclusion of orthodoxy. Right beliefs are simply superfluous. How we live is all that matters. Pragmatism reigns.

Presumably, if Bell or McLaren found a better 'way to live', they would dump Christianity and adopt that better way. This might explain why Bell was an official participant at the Seeds of Compassion conference in April 2008, with Hindu, Muslim, Jewish,

Buddhist and Sikh leaders and featuring 'His Holiness the Dalai Lama'.[18] According to their website:

The concluding session of Seeds of Compassion [was] a *Youth and Spiritual Connection Dialogue*. Global, national and local luminaries representing faiths from around the world [gathered] to discuss nurturing youth with spirituality [emphasis in the original].[19]

Perhaps Bell, who was one of the 'luminaries' and does not want to argue over beliefs, has found a better trampoline on which to bounce. If youth can be nurtured better by the Dalai Lama, or a Muslim imam, or a Zen Buddhist master, then trampoline upgrading would seem appropriate, since the big question for Bell, as he has stated, is not what is true but, 'Is the way of Jesus still the best possible way to live?' If a better way can be found, then Jesus' trampoline would need to be replaced by the better, higher-bouncing model. Since ultimately all that matters is what gives us a higher bounce, then what we believe is inconsequential and what the Dalai Lama has to offer might be superior.

'Is the way of Jesus *still* the *best possible* way to life?' (emphasis mine). It depends on how you define 'life'. Biblically there is no question — Jesus is 'the way, and the truth, and the life' (John 14:6). When Scripture speaks of spiritual life it is speaking of unity with God and, therefore, when Jesus says that 'no one comes to the Father but through Me' (John 14:6), he is telling us that true spiritual life is the opposite of spiritual death, which is separation from God. Life means being brought into a saving relationship with God. At times that might mean that experientially we are overwhelmed with the greatness of God and the joys of Christian living. At other times, life on this planet, even for the strongest believer, can be a great struggle with the forces of evil, a sinful world and our own flesh.

Scripture never minimizes these experiences, even though it redeems them (e.g. Rom. 5:1-10). What the Word does *not* do is invite us to the Father through the Son in order to experience a happier existence (a higher bounce) and then trade up if we can find a better deal elsewhere. Instead the invitation to know God is based on the truth that God is real and Jesus is the only way to union with the Father (Acts 4:12). The issue is not whether Jesus is the best possible way of living the 'good life', but that Jesus *is* the life and the *only* way to true life as defined as a relationship with God. If we follow Bell's formula a better way may seem to come along every so often. If we follow the biblical formula no such alternative is possible. When Jesus asked the apostles if they were going to follow the crowd and abandon him too, Peter replied, 'Lord, to whom shall we go? You have words of eternal life' (John 6:68). Peter saw that Jesus was the only option if someone wanted the truth that led to eternal life.

A blast from the past

McLaren, Bell and others write and speak winsomely about what they are offering, but history, not to mention Scripture, suggests that great caution must be exercised at this point. Murray reminds us that nineteenth-century 'liberal theology very rarely presented itself as being in opposition to Scripture. On the contrary, its exponents claimed the authority of the New Testament for the view that Christianity is life, not doctrine.'[20] Some, using this line of reasoning, like the eventual Archbishop of Canterbury William Temple, could say, 'An atheist who lives by love is saved by his faith in the God whose existence (under that Name) he denies.'[21] It was living by love that mattered, not what one believed about God. Schleiermacher went so far as to bar doctrinal preaching from the pulpit for 'experience, not teaching, is to be the object of the preacher'.[22]

As, theologically speaking, the twenty-first century seems to be an echo of the nineteenth, so too is the reaction of evangelicals. While there was a concerted effort on the part of some of the most conservative believers towards the end of the 1800s to combat liberalism,[23] many chose to hang back and express tolerance.

Murray reports, 'There were some who were unsure what to think, and in their uncertainty they erred on the side of neutrality and false charity. It was probably the attitude of this group which eventually allowed the new teaching to become so general.'[24] This is the error often being repeated today by well-intentioned evangelicals who don't want to make waves and who fear, above all things, that they might be called 'fundamentalists'. Historically, fundamentalists in America marched to the frontlines to do battle with the opposing liberalism of the early twentieth century. On the other hand, evangelicals in Great Britain took a more relaxed approach and unintentionally, as Murray would confirm, allowed liberalism ultimately to win the day. Much criticism has been launched at the fundamentalist movement — some of it deservedly — but arguably it is the fundamentalist who should be given much credit for the preservation of the evangelical faith in America.

Relevant and authentic

But just as great a concern to many evangelicals as being called by the dreaded name of 'fundamentalists' is being labelled 'not relevant', or lacking in authenticity. Being 'relevant' and 'authentic' are two buzzwords popular in many Christian circles today. Everyone wants to be relevant and authentic, although defining what these words mean often proves to be difficult. Some time ago I had lunch with a pastor from one of the best-known 'authentic' churches in America. Since this church is known world over for its authenticity and relevancy, and since it is has become the flagship church for these coveted features, I asked him to describe for me in what way his church members were authentic and relevant. I was especially curious about his answer within the context of my local church, which could be described as conservative, Bible-centred and basic.

The pastor stumbled around a bit, behaving as though he had never before heard such a question. Possibly I was the first person he had met who was dumb enough not to know what 'relevant' and 'authentic' mean (by the way, you will find the same response if you ask what it means to be 'missional', or what 'the kingdom' really is — two other buzzwords in postmodern church circles). Finally he told me that most of his people wear jeans to church, to which I replied that some of ours do too. He then said his people lived authentically in the community, to which I replied that many of ours do as well (although in theory you are not supposed to define a word by using the word). Upon further urging from me he then said that his people drink beer (I assume he did not mean during the church services themselves!). I am pretty sure that some of our people do too, but they don't talk about it (at least not when I'm around) and it surely would not be a badge of authenticity. I asked, 'Is that all you got?' But he was done and had nothing more to say.

Surely casual dress at church services and drinking alcohol are not the definition of either 'authentic' or 'relevant'? And I am sure this pastor could have provided some better descriptions of these concepts had he had more time to reflect. Still, from reading his church's literature and website I know that added to this list is the use of any form of music in church gatherings, no matter how godless or whether performed by unbelievers, use of foul and gutter language, sexually inappropriate comments and illustrations, and involvement in almost any form of entertainment and amusement which is attractive to unbelievers. As a matter of fact, I get the idea that 'relevancy' and 'authenticity' are terms being used today, at least by some, to describe what evangelicals of another generation called 'worldliness'.

'Worldliness' — now that is a word you won't often find in 'relevant' Christian literature and churches, except to make fun of 'prudish' Christians who still care about such things. Past generations of believers saw purity and separation from questionable activities as not only obedience to God (Rom. 12:2), but also a witness to unbelievers. Not that unbelievers necessarily understood or appreciated the Christian's desire for living a separated life (another old-fashioned term you won't hear in most Christian circles today), but they recognized that in many regards true Christians lived differently from the way they did (1 Peter 4:3-4). While this repelled and even infuriated some, it nevertheless served notice that Christ transformed the life and the lifestyle of those he regenerated.

It is this very thing against which many who cry 'relevancy' today have reacted. How, they ask, can we expect to draw people to Christ by modelling for them a lifestyle they find repugnant? If we are to win unbelievers to the Lord we must identify with them. We must show them that we enjoy the same things they do. They must be made to realize that Christians can drink and swear and dress like them, and can gamble and be foul and enjoy all the same forms of entertainment that non-Christians do. Living in this way, we are told, will be winsome to the unbeliever, for they will see in us an authentic life which is transparent and free from hypocrisy and smugness — characteristics that the unbeliever claims to see so universally in Christians. We are, after all, no different from them except that we believe in Christ. Emergent leader Jim Henderson, in a book co-authored with an atheist and sponsored by George Barna, writes, '[Unbelievers are] just like me, except they're not currently interested in Jesus to the same degree I am.'[25]

Certainly, the caricature of Christians as smug and hypocritical is sometimes realistic. Too often believers are afraid to admit their weaknesses and deficiencies. They may put on airs while they are struggling with the same things that all people do — sin, loneliness, disappointment, pain, etc. On this type of pretence we need to call a moratorium. But it is surely an overreaction to adopt a lifestyle characteristic of those who do not know the redeeming power of Christ in a misguided notion that we will attract them to the Lord as a result.

Truth and authority

What we are talking about ultimately concerns the issues of truth and authority — two concepts which emergent thinkers believe falsely come from the Enlightenment, not Scripture. As we have seen, postmodern church leaders, like those of liberalism in the past, have tried to drive a wedge between life and doctrine. If they are correct then what we believe does not matter; what matters are our experiences, our emotions and our behaviour. It needs to be clearly stated that no one I know is discounting the importance of 'life', but there are numerous things wrong with equating Christianity with life alone. For one thing, this reductionist approach is simply impossible. There is no life, good or bad, that does not stem from our beliefs. Even as emergent leaders such as McLaren and Bell decry doctrine, they are nevertheless teaching their own brand of theology. The very rejection of doctrine as one's basis for authority is itself a theological pronouncement. Conservatives may affirm ideas that emergents reject, but both are testifying to a system of beliefs. Emergents believe that many things the Bible teaches and evangelicals avow are not true, or at least not necessary for life and spiritual experience. One proclaims certain truths; the other rejects them — but both are expressing their approach to theology. It is merely word-play to speak of 'life, not doctrine'.

Our source of authority is another problematic issue with the life-versus-doctrine school of thought. Ultimately everyone has linked his or her beliefs and life to some concept of authority. For the biblical Christian that source is the Word of God. When Scripture speaks, and on whatever subject it speaks, it has the last word. All other voices are silenced in the presence of God's revelation. Our task as believers is to seek to understand what the Word teaches and apply it to our lives.

Some in the Christian community will challenge this idea head-on. They will tell us the Bible is an outdated book full of stories, myths and historical accounts that bear witness to God's revelation but that it is not itself the very revelation of God. It is a book written by men and, as such, its pronouncements and teachings can be seen as little more than sage advice which we are free to filter, adopting or rejecting according as this advice conforms to our own opinions. In this same vein others would make Scripture subservient to science, psychotherapy and modern thought. After all, the Bible is an ancient book and can hardly be expected to have much to say to citizens of Planet Earth in the twenty-first century. In both of these scenarios authority rests either in the individual or in the collective wisdom of men rather than the Word of God.

The average Christian follows neither of these scenarios, however. Most would pay lip service to the authority of Scripture, but in practice their real master (authority) is pragmatism. They would never deny the infallibility and the value of God's Word, but in reality 'what works', or at least what they think works, calls the shots. It is not that they have consciously rejected what God has revealed, but their default mode is what seems to be working at the moment.

And what seems to be working right now? On an ecclesiastical level the churches and para-church organizations that are most likely to be successful, if you define success in terms of money and attendance, are the very ones who are giving people what they want to hear rather than what God wants them to hear. People want to hear about how to be successful, how to have a happier marriage and how to feel good about themselves, as opposed to the biblical concepts of how to glorify God, how to have a godly marriage, how to deny self, how to take up one's cross and follow Christ. Since most Christians have the wrong goals for their lives, having derived them from conforming their thinking to the world rather than being transformed by the renewing of their minds (Rom. 12:2), it is not surprising that they live by the world's methodologies as well. Individual Christians who now want the same things the unbeliever wants must use the methods the unbeliever has created. When we have accepted that the purpose of life is being successful, popular, powerful, wealthy, having a healthy self-image, and so forth, the Scriptures have little to offer because these are not biblical categories. That is, God does not define true life in the same way the world does. The Lord has much to say about denying self, but nothing about loving self. He has much to say about joy, but nothing positive about amusing ourselves to death (as one author calls it). He offers loads of principles concerning finances, but little about how to be rich, and even warns about the desire for wealth (1 Tim. 6:9-10). The Bible is filled with ways of bringing honour to God and lifting up his greatness, but calls us to focus on personal humility (Luke 9:46-48).

We do not naturally think as God thinks. While regeneration changes our nature, it is a lifelong task to be 'transformed by the renewing of [our minds]' (Rom. 12:2) — a process never completed during our lifetime. It is not surprising to find that, since we so easily turn to the wrong sources (such as self) for understanding life, we also use the wrong means in our effort to find life (such as pragmatism). If life is defined as succeeding at what one does, then whatever enables one to succeed will become one's controlling influence (dare we say one's god?). Pragmatism therefore, simply because it seems to 'work', is dominating the Christian landscape today. Truth, as revealed in God's Word, is taking a backseat to the doctrine of 'what works'.

King Pragmatism is on the throne of too many lives and churches, but fortunately there is a means of overthrowing the king. Paul paved the way when he said that he was 'destroying speculations and every lofty thing raised up against the knowledge of God ... [and] taking every thought captive to the obedience of Christ' (2 Cor. 10:5). We must challenge our thinking with the revelation of God. We must allow the Word to have the first word and the last word in our lives. As Isaiah said to the ancient people of Israel, 'To the law and to the testimony! If they do not speak according to this word, it is because they have no dawn' (Isa. 8:20).

Conclusion

John Piper, in his excellent book *The Supremacy of God in Preaching*, writes of the need for preachers to be diligent in reminding their listeners of the grandeur of God, although most have no idea that such a message is important to them. The majority would rather hear 'relevant' sermons and will criticize the pastor who focuses on God and not on their personal 'felt needs'. 'Pastor Piper,' he has a critic complain, 'Can't you see your people are hurting? Can't you come down out of the heavens and get practical? Don't you realize what kind of people sit in front of you on Sunday?' To which Piper replies:

> The greatness and the glory of God are relevant. It does not matter if surveys turn up a list of perceived needs that does not include the supreme greatness of the sovereign God of grace. That is the deepest need. Our people are starving for God.[26]

George Gallup, in a book which explores spirituality in the twenty-first century, suggests, 'The problem is not so much that people do not believe anything; it is that they believe everything.'[27] He sees this as a problem for the foreseeable future because 'the emphasis [at this time] is on a desired feeling or fleeting moment of wonder, not on understanding truths with a larger view or power to truly transform'.[28]

Not too long ago, if your child wanted a stuffed animal, you went to some local retail outlet and bought one off the shelf. While there may have been a large number of possibilities, still the options were limited to the stuffed animals in stock. Enter 'Build a Bear' franchises, which have popped up in many places. At Build a Bear children can create their own stuffed animals. They can be as creative as they like, for Build a Bear allows children to be sovereign over their own creations, leaving the toy store with a unique toy animal unlike anyone else's. The only question is: 'What does the child want in a stuffed animal?' But what may be desirable in a fuzzy friend is not desirable when it comes to God and the Christian faith. Neither the Lord nor the faith is left to our desires or designs. While there is much diversity within the body of Christ, there is only one Lord and one faith (Eph. 4:5). We are not free to 'build a God' or 'build a faith'. The one true God and the one true faith have been handed down to us in the Word. We must reject the temptation to be our own creators and humbly accept that which the Lord has revealed to us. Pragmatism, the god of 'what works', is a creation of our own imagination and ingenuity. We must rest in the true God of the Word.

6

The New Atheism

There is much discussion lately about the so-called 'new atheism'. This seems to be an odd term, given the fact that there are not very many ways that a person can spin atheism — old atheism denied the existence of God and new atheism does the same, so what is the difference? There is a sense in which even old atheism is new; after all, until the Enlightenment of the eighteenth century real atheists were hard to find. It is true that practical atheism can be traced throughout history. Psalm 14:1 speaks of such a man, termed a 'fool', who says in his heart, 'There is no God.' Most see this fool not as a philosophical atheist who mentally denies the existence of God, but as one who lives as though God does not exist, even though intellectually he knows better. Of course the practical atheist is far more common than those who adopt atheism as a worldview. Most people, especially in the Western world, give God a nod (92% of Americans say they believe in God), then go about living their lives as though God were non-existent. Unfortunately, too many Christians fall into this category (but that is another matter).

Biblically speaking, the whole issue of atheism is problematic. Romans 1:18-23 indicates that God has situated his creation so as to be a constant reminder of his existence. That a few deny this evidence does not negate the fact that to some degree they know better. And Romans 2:15 confirms what we already know to be true, that God has placed in the hearts of each of us a moral standard — his fingerprints are found on our conscience. A human is not just another mammal; we are different; we bear the marks of the image of God, and on some level even self-avowed atheists know that this is so. But such is the hardening of the flesh and the blinding power of the Evil One that some can turn their backs on what they intuitively know to be true and create a worldview that eliminates God altogether. That new atheism is gaining traction among many such people is evidenced by the sales of this genre of books and the attention afforded to its leaders. More of this in a moment, but first let's turn to old atheism for a backdrop.

The four horsemen + four more

Albert Mohler identifies Friedrich Nietzsche, Karl Marx, Charles Darwin and Sigmund Freud as what he calls the 'four horsemen' of old atheism.[1] These nineteenth-century men have had an incredible impact on modern society as each of them shaped his respective field around his atheistic views: Nietzsche influenced philosophy and is a sort of prototype today for many postmodernists; Marx changed how much of the world understood society and government; Darwin rewrote the scientific textbooks; and Freud redefined the human mind. It would be hard to find anyone in the Western world who has had more influence on how we think and live today than these four men; each of them, including his body of work and influence, was largely the product of his denial of the existence of God.

Friedrich Nietzsche might be worth a little attention as he is representative of the views of old atheism. Nietzsche is famous for his statement that 'God is dead'. By that Nietzsche was not so much saying that God had actually lived at one point and had died, but that God was no longer needed by society. There was apparently a time when a belief in God was necessary in order to bring about moral order within the human race, but it was now time for people to grow up and move on. Once it was accepted that God was dead there would inevitably be an adjustment period which would prove painful for mankind — after all, why behave morally if there is no God and no eternal reckoning? — but ultimately something far better would emerge.

Nietzsche knew, however, that with the loss of an absolute would come nihilism and despair. Without God where would humans find their reason to live, their purpose, their foundation for morals and values? Nietzsche took this problem seriously and worked to replace God with what he called the 'will to power'. Once God was disposed of, men could finally stop wasting time on religion and turn to self-development and to the value of the world itself. Nietzsche believed that the shadows of God would linger for a long time, possibly even for thousands of years, as the transition from a theistic-based world to an atheistic one would be painful; nevertheless this transition must be completed for the good of all. Still, in Nietzsche, as with most of those representing old atheism, there is a sense of loss. Nietzsche is right — despair is hard to shake off if there is no God. As a result, Nietzsche and many other early atheists lived with unresolved tension between their philosophical systems, which denied God, and the actual reality of living in a universe which seemed to need God in order to survive and have purpose.

Fast forward to the new atheism and its four horsemen (according to Mohler) — Richard Dawkins, Daniel Dennett, Sam Harris and Christopher Hitchens.[2] These men claim to have moved beyond the nihilism of a godless universe and are living Nietzsche's dream, framing the world around the creation (which of course has no creator) rather than around the Creator himself. The new four horsemen are thrilled with their beliefs and eager to spread their atheistic gospel. They want converts and they are aggressively taking their message to the masses in popular, easy-to-digest lectures, books and articles. Richard Dawkins makes clear his intention when he writes early in his book *The God Delusion*, 'If this book works as I intend, religious readers who open it will be atheists when they put it down.'[3] This evangelistic fervour has gone mainstream in some places. For example, the American Humanist Association launched an advertising campaign for Christmas 2008 in Washington DC, in which signs were placed on buses that read, 'Why believe in a god? Just be good for goodness sake.'[4] In Britain a similar campaign (orchestrated by the British Humanist Association) placed messages on London buses stating, 'There's probably no God. Now stop worrying and enjoy your life.'[5] These groups define humanism as 'a progressive philosophy of life that, without theism, affirms our responsibility to lead ethical lives of value to self and humanity'.[6] This is the good news that the new atheists want the world to hear.

Major themes within new atheism

If the new atheists want followers, how are they packaging their gospel to attract disciples? What is their methodology? Allow me to illustrate their agenda using Dawkins, the best-known of this new breed of atheists, as my source.

They attack Christianity

While atheism is the denial of any form of theism, it is Christianity which is largely in its sights. Perhaps this is because Dawkins and company know that the majority of their readers are most likely to live in Christian cultures, or perhaps it is because Christianity presents the most formidable argument against their view. At any rate, Dawkins reserves his most venomous attacks for the God of the Bible. He states:

> The God of the Old Testament is arguably the most un-pleasant character in all fiction: jealous and proud of it; a petty, unjust, unforgiving control-freak; a vindictive, blood-thirsty ethnic cleanser; a misogynistic, homophobic, racist, infanticidal, genocidal, filicidal, pestilential, megalomaniacal, sadomasochistic, capriciously malevolent bully.[7]

And the God of the New Testament fares no better — perhaps worse. Even though the God of the New Testament seems slightly more admirable than that of the Old Testament, Dawkins suggests:

> There are other teachings in the New Testament that no good person should support. I refer especially to the central doctrine of Christianity: that of 'atonement' for 'original sin'. This teaching, which lies at the heart of New Testament theology, is almost as morally obnoxious as the story of Abraham setting out to barbecue Isaac.[8]

From the perspective of the new atheists the stories and teachings of the Bible reveal a God so odious as to be unbelievable.

Belief in God is silly

On a scale of one to seven, with one representing 100% certainty of the existence of God and seven standing for 100% certainty that he does not exist, even Dawkins places himself at six, which technically makes him an agnostic rather than an atheist. However, before we say, 'See! I told you so,' Dawkins explains himself: 'I am agnostic only to the extent that I am agnostic about fairies at the bottom of the garden.'[9] This seems to be the style of the new atheists. Lacking a good case, they resort to berating and ridiculing theists. Not only is belief in God on the same level as belief in fairies, but Dawkins dismisses out of hand the evidences presented by Christians throughout the ages as being baseless. He doesn't even interact in any meaningful way with the thoughts presented by Aquinas and others, implying that such arguments are unworthy of discussion and not taken seriously by anyone today[10] (which is not true, as we shall see). Only the teleological argument, that design implies a Designer, gets any attention at all and that cursory. Yet I still recall hiking through the wilderness of Alaska and coming across a fire ring. My initial, and certainly correct, assumption was that someone had camped in that spot and arranged twenty or so stones in a circle. It never crossed my mind that evolution over a period of millions of years had created that fire ring — and I am willing to wager it would have not crossed the mind of Dawkins either. It amazes me that people who would see a designer behind a fire ring can so casually dismiss a Designer behind the universe, but such is the mind-set of the atheist. Dawkins' best retort to the teleological argument seems to be that, if God designed the universe, who designed God? Unable to unravel this question to his satisfaction, Dawkins concludes that the teleological argument is lame.[11]

Recent and respected theists, those not subject to chasing fairies around the garden, are similarly dismissed. Of C. S. Lewis's argument that Jesus must have been either a liar, a lunatic or Lord, Dawkins simply says, '[Lewis] should have known better.'[12] Dawkins suggests that Jesus could have been sincerely mistaken instead. However, it seems to me that such a 'mistake' would have placed our Saviour firmly in the lunatic category (as Lewis suggests), just as we would place any of our acquaintances who made such a claim. No normal person mistakenly thinks he is God.

Dawkins furthers his argument by stating that theistic scientists are either deluded or senile or out of touch with the research. After all, of the scientists who are members of the National Academy of Sciences, only 7% believe in a personal God.[13]

Natural selection to the rescue

Sidestepping for the moment the issue of who created God, both theists and atheists are left with the question of who or what created everything around us. Theists of any sort would look to a deity powerful enough to form the universe out of nothing. The atheist, rejecting such a deity, must find something as powerful as God which nevertheless remains impersonal. That something is natural selection. Over and over in *The God Delusion* Dawkins turns to natural selection as the saviour of his system:

Darwin and his successors have shown how living creatures, with their spectacular statistical improbability and appearance of design, have evolved by slow, gradual degrees from simple beginnings. We can now safely say that the illusion of design in living creatures is just that — an illusion.[14]

Dawkins is very sensitive to the charge that natural selection is just a glorified version of luck and chance. Responding to the accusation that the probability of life originating on earth apart from God is as likely as a hurricane sweeping through a scrapyard and forming a Boeing 747 (a favourite of creationists, we are told), Dawkins retorts:

This... [is] an argument that could be made only by some-body who doesn't understand the first thing about natural selection: somebody who thinks natural selection is a theory of chance whereas — in the relevant sense of chance — it is the opposite.[15]

If natural selection is not a theory of chance, exactly what is it? Dawkins states, 'It not only explains the whole of life; it also raises our consciousness to the power of science to explain how organized complexity can emerge from simple beginnings without any deliberate guidance.'[16] Excuse me, but this sounds like random chance to me, although Dawkins is ready to explain:

What is it that makes natural selection succeed as a solution to the problem of improbability, where chance and design both fail at the starting gate? The answer is that natural se-lection is a cumulative process, which breaks the problem of improbability up into small pieces. Each of the small pieces is slightly improbable, but not prohibitively so. When large numbers of these slightly improbable events are stacked up in a series, the end product of the accumulation is very very improbable indeed, improbable enough to be far beyond the reach of chance. It is these end products that form the sub-jects of the creationist's wearisomely recycled argument. The creationist completely misses the point, because he ... insists on treating the genesis of statistical improbability as a single, one-off event. He doesn't understand the power of accumulation.[17]

The argument, then, is that the end product (say a tree, or an animal, or woman) would not be possible if it was a 'single, one-off event'. A single random act of creation is beyond the possibility of chance, but if the end product is the result of a multitude of random acts of creation, each building on the last, then virtually anything is possible. The magic, if I could call it that, lies in the 'power of accumulation'. Dawkins accuses the creationist of being someone who 'doesn't understand the first thing about natural selection: somebody who thinks natural selection is a theory of chance', but it seems to me that the creationist understands all too well the theory behind natural selection. Whether creation is a 'one-off' chance action, or an accumulation of millions of acts of chance (per created object), it is still chance. And by atheistic definition and necessity, natural selection must be unguided acts of chance since there is no God residing in the universe.

Of course the evolutionist believes that natural selection is not entirely random and will always, eventually, produce a better end product, but to hold to such a belief the atheist must ascribe to natural selection the very attributes that he denies to God — omniscience and omnipotence. To the atheist, natural selection, with its power of accumulation chance theory, becomes his god.

Next up is the tricky issue of how life began. For even the most devoted evolutionist the origin of life is virtually inexplicable. Natural selection cannot deliver the atheist when it comes to origins because there was originally nothing for natural selection to operate on. Dawkins skirts the issue of the origin of organic material by complaining that it is harder to explain the existence of God than the eternal existence of matter. But once this premise is accepted, what would be the scenario under which life would form? In response Dawkins propounds a theory he calls the 'Goldilocks zone'. That is, earth just happened to be situated in the universe at precisely the perfect place at the perfect time (the Goldilocks zone) 'in ways that singled it out for the evolution of life'.[18]

If this sounds a bit like luck to you, you would be correct, and ironically Dawkins agrees. As a matter of fact, there apparently is a lot of luck floating around in the evolutionary pond. 'It may be,' Dawkins admits, 'the origin of life is not the only major gap in the evolutional story that is bridged by sheer luck'; the origin of human-type cells and consciousness is as well.[19] This element of luck does not diminish Dawkins' faith in natural selection, for he is convinced that 'natural selection works because it is a cumulative one-way street to improvement. It needs some luck to get started, and the billions of planets' anthropic principle grants it that luck.'[20] Incredibly Dawkins sees the luck factor necessary for natural selection as being vastly superior to intellectual design by an omniscient Creator. Indeed, he attributes the 'amazing blindness' of theists to 'the fact that many people have not had their consciousness raised, as biologists have, by natural selection and its power to tame improbability'.[21] The arrogance in such a statement is self-evident, but such arrogance is, in the final analysis, all the atheists have.

Atheists are good people too

One of the strongest arguments by Christians against atheism is that atheism provides no foundation for decent and moral living. If God does not exist, then no final authority exists which can arbitrate between right and wrong. Additionally there is no final judgment facing those who do evil. In the light of these ideas Christians often assume that atheists will ultimately and consistently live out the conclusions of their beliefs, resulting in nihilism and anarchy. Tim Wildmon, president of the American Family Association asks, 'How do we define "good" if we don't believe in God? God in his Word, the Bible, tells us what's good and bad and right and wrong. If we are each ourselves defining what's good, it's going to be a crazy world.'[22]

To this issue Dawkins devotes an entire chapter. His strongest rebuttal is that there does not exist any significant difference between the behaviour of Christians and that of non-Christians.[23]

Good behaviour is ensured by our own selfish need to survive and the reciprocal altruism ('You scratch my back, and I'll scratch yours') that natural selection has hot-wired into the human creature.[24] Dawkins then concludes that 'We do not need God in order to be good — or evil.'[25] The new atheists have concluded that they really have no need of God.

A defence of theism

Fundamentally, the new atheism is different from other forms of atheism, not in its beliefs, but in its joyful evangelistic zeal to smash all opposing views and establish Darwinian evolution as the one claim to truth left standing. It is an unapologetically modernistic approach in a supposedly postmodern world, yet it is winning many adherents. For example, billboards were erected in November 2008 throughout Denver by an atheist group called Colorado Coalition of Reason. The billboards read, 'Don't believe in God? You're not alone.'[26] The new atheism is aggressive and out for converts. It has declared outright war on all forms of theism in general and Christianity in particular. Some people will be taken in by all the rhetoric, logic and efforts by Dawkins and company, but upon closer examination it is discovered that their arguments don't hold water; they leak at several points — scientifically, philosophically and spiritually.

Scientifically

Richard Dawkins is an eminent professor at Oxford University and considered one of the most distinguished scientists in the world today, yet his book *The God Delusion* is faulted scientifically even by his own peers — both Christian and non-Christian. Perhaps the most helpful critique from a Christian perspective is that of Alistair McGrath, himself an Oxford professor of historical theology and a fellow scientist with a degree in molecular biophysics. While McGrath respects Dawkins as a scientist (and, sadly, accepts some form of theistic evolution), he believes that, in attempting to propagate his atheistic views, Dawkins left the evidence of science at the door and launched into a fundamentalist rant. According to McGrath, in his own book *The Dawkins Delusion?*, Dawkins misrepresents his sources, stretches the facts, makes up unpersuasive pseudoscientific ideas to bolster his position and in general simply does not prove his case.

Science, as Dawkins knows, cannot prove or disprove God. It can, however, examine the evidence and make various hypotheses. Given the evidence, which of the following hypotheses best makes sense of all we see and observe around us?

• The theory of evolution, which embraces random chance, omniscient but impersonal natural selection and a 'Goldilocks zone' in which our planet, and life as we know it, formed; or
• A creator God who wisely brought all things into existence and placed in balance the highly complicated and integrated universe that we can study scientifically and enjoy physically, emotionally and spiritually.

The new atheists have placed their bets on natural selection and evolutionary theory, but they know these things cannot be verified. Dawkins himself admits that Darwinism, as he understands it today, may radically change and even be disproved in the future. He writes, 'New facts may come to light which will force our successors ... to abandon Darwinism or modify it beyond recognition.'[27] Yet Dawkins gamely clings tightly to his evolutionary theories and belittles anyone he considers foolish enough, or deluded enough, to believe in God.

Atheists are placing their faith in a theory that they can be reasonably certain will not be the same a hundred years from now, while Christians place their faith in a God who claims to be 'the same, yesterday, today and forever' (Heb. 13:8). Ultimately, the new atheists' rejection of God is not scientific; it is philosophical and spiritual.

Philosophically

Alister McGrath claims, '*The God Delusion* is a work of theater rather than scholarship — a fierce, rhetorical assault on religion and passionate plea for it to be banished to the lunatic fringes of society, where it can do no harm.'[28]

He is not alone; even Marxist scholar Terry Eagleton attacks Dawkins for his naïve view that Christians live by blind faith void of evidence. He writes:

> Imagine someone holding forth on biology whose only knowledge of the subject is the Book of British Birds, and you have a rough idea of what it feels like to read Richard Dawkins on theology... For mainstream Christianity reason, argument and honest doubt have always played an integral role in belief.[29]

Christian philosopher Alvin Plantinga challenges Dawkins' basic understanding of philosophical and theological issues involving theism. In rather demeaning words Plantinga states, 'Why, you might say that some of his forays into philosophy are at best sophomoric, but that will be unfair to sophomores.'[30]

The new atheist has accepted by faith (blind or otherwise) the proposition that God does not exist, that the universe has no design or purpose — anything that seems to indicate design or purpose is just an appearance of such — and that natural selection reigns supreme. This leads to spiritual implications that I will cover below, but for now we need to think carefully about the evidence. Neither the atheist nor the theist can prove scientifically that God exists — both must express faith to a certain degree. Nevertheless, both must come to their conclusions based upon an examination of the evidence that they have before them. The atheist attempts to take the high ground here, claiming that science is on his side for, after all, according to Dawkins, as stated earlier, only about 7% of scientists in the National Academy of Sciences believe in a personal God.[31] Does that mean the case is closed? Not so fast! Another well-known survey of scientists in

1997 found that 40% believed in God, 40% did not and 20% were uncertain.[32] The difference, as with many surveys, seems to be in how the questions were presented. Nevertheless, the point is well made: even scientists, handling the same physical evidence, come to different conclusions about the existence of God. It cannot simply be assumed that some scientists are stupid and others are clever.

Apparently the evidence does not constitute an open-and-shut case for Darwinism even among scientists, as the new atheists would have us believe. Nor is the evidence of God as weak as Dawkins and company would conjecture. While Dawkins dismisses out of hand the time-honoured evidence for the existence of God, Alvin Plantinga, perhaps the most influential Christian apologist and philosopher alive today, believes there are two or three dozen good arguments for the existence of God.[33] These include the fact that something exists rather than nothing, the probability of the universe being so perfectly fine-tuned that humans can exist, the regularity of nature, the fact that purpose exists in the heart of mankind, and so forth. Some of these arguments are closely aligned to the historical arguments that Dawkins debunks without engagement, but that have been rethought and updated by some of Christianity's best thinkers.

Apologist William Lane Craig has written a book on this subject (*Reasonable Faith*) and summarizes some of his arguments in an article published in 2008.[34] For example, the *cosmological* argument is based on the observation that everything that exists has a cause or explanation for its existence, and the most plausible cause is God. The *moral* argument asserts that the very existence and recognition of moral values (which even most atheists accept) are powerful clues that one exists who has ordained moral values. And the *teleological* argument — that a design requires a designer — is still a powerful piece of evidence for those who approach the clues with an open mind. The modern debate surrounding this argument focuses on the fine-tuning of the universe that allows life as we know it — what Dawkins calls the 'Goldilocks zone'. The updated teleological argument has three premises:

1. The fine-tuning of the universe is due either to physical necessity, chance, or design.
2. It is not due to physical necessity or chance.
3. Therefore, it is due to design.

The first premise is just a list of the options. Premise number two is where most of the debate rages. Physical necessity seems impossible to accept and chance seems ridiculous in the light of the complexity of the universe. If physical necessity and chance are dismissed as incredible, that leaves design. But who is the designer? The most obvious conclusion is God.

Of course this does not convince the new atheists. Dawkins, it seems to me, would agree with all three premises but concludes that the designer is natural selection. He examines the same evidence as the theists and concludes that natural selection (which he denies is really blind chance) is the omniscient designer of the cosmos. While he cannot prove this, Dawkins' standard response is that his faith in natural selection is more plausible than belief in God. But is it? Dawkins' position runs counter to every observation in life. Nothing is created without a creator. Chance occurrences rarely produce anything of value, and when they do the outcome is simple, random and non-recurring. It is inconceivable to believe that the complexity found in virtually everything from cells to planets is the product of little more than billions of accidents over billions of years. Does faith placed in chance (and the bottom line is that natural selection is nothing more than chance) seem superior to belief in the existence of God? Both the atheist and the theist interact with the same information, yet they draw different conclusions. Why? Because they begin with different presuppositions. This leads us directly into the spiritual issues involved.

Before we move to the spiritual dimension, and the most powerful argument for the existence of God, let's say a word about postmodernism. Since we are constantly being told that we live in a postmodern world, which does not reason from logic and is not interested in proofs and evidence, but rather focuses on the metaphysical, Christians are being told we should just share our story and hold a conversation (as per the emergent church). We are told that rational arguments simply won't work and are out of place. But are they? It seems to me that our culture is postmodern only when it comes to religion and philosophy. When the rubber really meets the road we are still highly modern people. Lane writes:

> In fact, a postmodern culture is an impossibility; it would be utterly unlivable. People are not relativistic when it comes to matters of science, engineering, and technology; rather, they are relativistic and pluralistic in matters of religion and ethics. But, of course, that's not postmodernism; that's modernism! That's just old-line verificationism, which held that anything you can't prove with your five senses is a matter of personal taste. We live in a culture that remains deeply modernist.[35]

I find it truly interesting in our supposedly postmodern culture that the undeniably modernistic new atheism has caught such a wave. Perhaps the architects of postmodern Christianity (i.e. the emerging/emergent leaders) should take note.

Spiritually

Having said all of this, when we return to Scripture we see that the Lord always views the rejection of God, either in total or in practice, as a spiritual matter. More than that, it is a rebellion against the clear evidence that God has placed in the world around us, as well as in our hearts. Early atheism seemed to recognize that if you move God out of the equation you leave a huge vacuum — actually more than one. Scientifically, the universe is left without a first cause — a Creator — and thus a new theory had to fill the gap, which evolution has attempted to do. But, primarily, without God we are left with a spiritual and moral vacuum. If God does not exist then why do right instead of wrong? Why, for example, should we care for the weak and the poor instead of exterminating them and thus freeing our society of the burden they produce? This is actually something of a problem for Darwinism and its 'survival of the fittest' axiom. If the strong bolster the gene pool and the weak diminish it then, according to the evolutionary theory, would not pouring resources into the survival of the weak actually be counter-productive to the existence of the human race? And if there is not a moral absolute in the form of God to regulate the conduct of human nature, who is to say that genocide of a race, or starvation of the poor, or murder of the disabled, is wrong? Ultimately a society devoid of God will come to such conclusions, as has been seen in communistic countries such as China and the former Soviet Union.

One of the things that distinguish older forms of atheism from new atheism is that early atheism recognized these facts and lamented, while new atheism rejects them and rejoices. For example, Jean-Paul Sartre, in his existential novel *Nausea*, tells the tale of a man who finally comes to grips with the idea that nothing that we do really matters for the very reason that *we* do not really matter. Sartre's summary of life is: 'Every existing thing is born without reason, prolongs itself out of weakness and dies by chance.'[36] It is the goal of the novel to prove this thesis; therefore Sartre, through the fictional character Antoine Roquentin, system-atically examines everything from religion to education to work to love and pronounces them all meaningless. When Roquentin looks inside himself he finds nothing. From this comes his despair; everything is absurd. He is an accident, a product of chance, and therefore nothing matters. Similarly, Albert Camus, in his novel *The Fall,* writes about a man who watched a woman drown and did nothing to save her. In his atheistic philosophy of life he could see no advantage for this woman either to live or to die and, since attempting to save her could endanger his own life, he simply ignored her and went home. But something deep inside would not leave him alone. The guilt began to eat away at his conscience. Intellectually he could discern no reason for this awful remorse, but his heart simply would not give him peace. Still, the experience did not change him or bring him to God. Instead he was able to dismiss the whole incident as inconsequential because his philosophy of life informed him that nothing really matters.

Since the older atheists '[suppressed] the truth in unrighteousness' (Rom. 1:18) by ignoring the outer witness of natural revelation (Rom. 1:18-20) and the inner witness of conscience (Rom. 2:14-15), God seemingly 'gave them over' (Rom. 1:24,26,28) to despair, or at least to a grave sense of loss. When the new atheists do the same things God appears to be giving them over to a sense of euphoria and intellectual blindness. In an interview with a friend Richard Dawkins talks about people not having any purpose if God does not exist. His friend retorts, 'Well, I don't think we're for anything. We're just products of evolution. You can say, "Gee, your life must be pretty bleak if you don't think there's a purpose." But I'm anticipating having a good lunch.' And Dawkins happily confirms that they did have a good lunch.[37] Where the older atheists were driven closer to despair over lack of purpose, the new atheists are content with a good lunch — and would recommend you have one, too. The issues haven't changed much, but the mood has.

Dawkins may joyfully accept that man has no real purpose, yet he accepts, and seems compelled to explain, why people have a disposition towards religion and moral behaviour without the existence of a personal God. Believing, as he does, that 'religion is so wasteful, so extravagant; and Darwinian selection habitually targets and eliminates waste', and 'knowing that we are products of Darwinian evolution, we should ask what pressure or pressures exerted by natural selection originally favoured the impulse to religion'.[38] Religion just does not make sense to an evolutionist. Dawkins concludes that some religious ideas might survive because of absolute merit[39] — that is, they somehow help our species to survive: 'There are circumstances — not particularly rare — in which genes ensure their own selfish survival by influencing organisms to behave altruistically.'[40] That is, moral notions and behaviour, sometimes stemming from religious ideas, are nothing more than the outworking of our selfish genes which natural selection has provided for us so that we will survive as a species.

This places the new atheists on the horns of a dilemma. On the one hand, we are accidents of nature; on the other, we are creatures with morals and values. The atheistic thinker Stephen Jay Gould wrote:

> We are here because one odd group of fishes had a peculiar fin anatomy that could transform into legs for terrestrial creatures; because comets struck the earth and wiped out dinosaurs, thereby giving mammals a chance not otherwise available... We may yearn for a 'higher' answer — but none exists. This explanation, though superficially troubling, if not terrifying, is ultimately liberating and exhilarating. We cannot read the meaning of life passively in the facts of nature. We must construct answers for ourselves...[41]

Since there is no higher answer as to why we are here, and since our very existence is accidental, then why do we have this sense of right and wrong, and why do we often act out this moral compulsion? The atheist must invent a theory in which unselfish and altruistic people survived in greater numbers and so perpetuated their unselfish genes. Yet even the atheists get lost in their own arguments. Dawkins, as we have seen, believes we survive on account of our 'selfish genes'. According to this view, selfish genes somehow created unselfish behaviour, which has allowed morally skewed people to multiply. Even more problematic is the fact that no one can explain where and how these genes (whether selfish or unselfish) originated in the first humans. When the evolutionist looks at nature he cannot help but recognize that it is a ruthless, violent place. The strong prey on the weak; life is unfair; pain and fear often rule. But the same evolutionist, at least of the new atheists' variety, recognizes that it is wrong for humans to behave in the same way as all other creatures in nature behave. They concoct strange and convoluted theories to get around the obvious. How much better the biblical account explains what we clearly observe around us and in us! The apostle Paul provides a reminder of what we already know:

> ... that which is known about God is evident within them; for God made it evident to them. For since the creation of the world His invisible attributes, His eternal power and divine nature, have been clearly seen, being understood through what has been made, so that they are without excuse (Rom. 1:19-20).

The new atheists, many of whom are scientists and have looked deeply into our created universe, have chosen to reject what they have clearly seen and observed in nature and in their own hearts, 'professing to be wise', and in the process 'they became fools' (Rom. 1:22). Whenever mankind chooses not to 'honor ... God or give thanks' to him, they suffer the fate of futile speculations and a foolish and darkened heart (Rom. 1:21). Nowhere is this more evident than with the new atheists, who have refused to bow the knee before the almighty Creator and have suffered the fate of being given over by him to their idols (Rom. 1:24-28). Ultimately the issues surrounding the new atheism are not scientific and they are not even philosophical; they are spiritual. In rejecting the 'clearly seen' evidence of God they have reaped the consequences of foolish and darkened hearts predisposed to believe the lie.

Conclusion

One of the mystifying things about the new atheism is that its cheerleaders are eager to make converts. We have to wonder why? It is one thing to believe that we, and the whole universe, are products of billions of little accidents governed by the apparently omniscient but impersonal power of natural selection, but why be so enthusiastic to destroy theism and spread your own ideas devoid of God? Could it be fear? Atheists from Nietzsche to Marx have assured future generations that theism would die a natural death in due time. But now here we are decades later and religion is stronger than ever. It has not gone away, and, with the collapse of Communism and the renewed interest in Christianity in Africa and Latin America, atheism has been losing, not gaining, ground. It is for this reason that Alister McGrath suggests that Dawkins' *The God Delusion* (the most influential book in the new atheists' arsenal):

> ... seems more designed to reassure atheists whose faith is faltering than to engage fairly or rigorously with religious believers and others seeking for truth... It is this deep, unsettling anxiety about the future of atheism that explains the 'high degree of dogmatism' and 'aggressive rhetorical style' of this new secular fundamentalism. Fundamentalism arises when a worldview feels it is in danger, lashing out at its enemies when it fears its own future is threatened.[42]

Part II

THE WAY BACK

7

A Renewed Confidence in the Word of God

Emergent spokesman Brian McLaren calls for the evangelical community to get over its love affair with certainty. He writes, 'Drop any affair you may have with certainty, proof, argument — and replace it with dialogue, conversation, intrigue, and search.'[1] Are we to take McLaren seriously? If so, then the best way to get over our love affair with certainty, according to McLaren, would be to replace it with uncertainty, or more commonly, mystery. It is definitely in vogue at this point in church history to assert categorically that we cannot be certain about anything. Of course, the irony of such certainty about uncertainty is obvious. But, much like impossible political promises, when statements are left unanalysed and unchallenged they tend to be uncritically absorbed by the minds of some people, often resulting in great harm.

It is important, then, that we give careful thought to the recent love affair with uncertainty. What are its origins? Is it really something new? Does it line up with the claims of Scripture? How should the people of God respond?

Inroads of uncertainty

There is little doubt that those espousing an 'uncertain', or mystical, brand of Christianity, as found in the emergent church and similar groups, are merely mimicking postmodern philosophy, which has permeated much of the Western world. Postmodernism,[2] which is still taking form and simultaneously has grown tiresome, is best known for its pronouncement of uncertainty. Knowable absolute and universal truth is denied, even despised, in the postmodern system. Christian thinker Os Guinness offers the following definition of postmodernism:

> Postmodernism is a movement and a mood as much as a clear set of ideas, so it often feels as if it is everywhere and nowhere. Doubtless, this means it is blamed for too much as well as too little. There are, of course, telltale fingerprints that postmodernism leaves on all it touches — the rejection of truth and objective standards of right and wrong, the leveling of authorities, the elevation of the autonomous self as the sole arbiter of life and reality, the equalizing of cultures, the promotion of image over character, the glorifying of power...[3]

As postmodernism has encroached on our society it is becoming more and more common to see its views reflected in many areas of evangelicalism. For example, theologian Donald Bloesch shows that postmodernism has left its mark on him when he writes, 'Scripture is authoritative by virtue of its relation to the living Word, not by virtue of its truthfulness as such.'[4] Elsewhere he says, 'The knowledge of faith is not an empirical objectifying knowledge but a knowledge in which we are lifted above reason and sense into communion with the living God.'[5] In a rather convoluted manner Bloesch is challenging a rationalistic perception of Scripture, which teaches that the Bible provides propositional truth and a common-sense approach to the understanding of life, and replacing it with a postmodern, mystical understanding.

Others have been clearer; for example, Brian McLaren believes conservatives have entirely missed the Bible's purpose and message and, therefore, 'Hardly anyone in conservative churches actually encounters the Bible any more.'[6] As a result, those of a postmodern bent, we are told, 'find the doctrines and principles [drawn from Scripture] as interesting as grass clippings'.[7] This is because conservatives, according to McLaren, 'have conquered the text, captured the meaning, removed all mystery, stuffed it and preserved it for posterity, like a taxidermist with a deer head'.[8] But even McLaren's friend and co-author, Tony Campolo, sees the danger of this mystical approach to the Scriptures. In response to the thoughts of McLaren as quoted above, Campolo writes:

> Most biblical scholars would contend that the apostle Paul's theological propositions have largely defined traditional Christianity... Brian may have bought into postmodern thinking just a little too much for me. As I see it, Jacques Derrida, the famous postmodern deconstructionist philosopher, and his followers contend that the text of Scripture has no single interpretation; instead the Bible should be read as though it was a Rorschach test. They tell us to see in the text whatever meaning we want to impose on it. They tell us that no single interpretation should be considered objectively valid. The text, say these postmodernists, has a life of its own — and once it is written, the reader provides the meaning. To me, that approach to the Bible has inherent dangers.[9]

Campolo, certainly no conservative, is nevertheless correct. Once we decide that the Bible is primarily the means of a mystical encounter with God, rather than God's truth revealed to man which is 'profitable for teaching, for reproof, for correction, for training in righteousness; so that the man of God may be adequate, equipped for every good work' (2 Tim. 3:16-17), the purpose of God's revelation changes. Scripture can be twisted to mean anything we want it to mean. The meaning of the revelation is not important; what matters is our supposed encounter with God. There is no question that we encounter God in the Bible, for as Jesus said, he came to 'explain' God to us (John 1:18), and Hebrews 1:2 tells us that God has spoken to us 'in His Son'. My contention is that we encounter God *in the truth that he reveals*. John said that his greatest joy was knowing that his 'children [were] walking in the truth' (3 John 4). The Bible offers more than claims to truth and propositions, but it does not offer less.

The product of uncertainty

A friend of mine who is a physician compares this postmodern/ mystical approach to the AIDS virus. He tells me:

Postmodernism attacks true Christianity's defense system, the truth (including God's Word), denying it exists or at least that it can be known with any degree of certainty. Like the AIDS virus, which leaves the body subject to all manner of infections and malignancies, postmodernism leaves Christianity with all manner of heresies if not apostasy.[10]

This disease of uncertainty has produced a very ill patient. A report entitled *Crisis in America's Churches: Bible Knowledge at All-Time Low*[11] reveals a startling picture of the evangelical church. Below are some of the findings by George Barna and other researchers:

• The most widely known Bible verse among adult and teen believers is: 'God helps those who help themselves' — which, by the way, is not in the Bible.
• Less than one out of every ten believers possesses a biblical worldview as the basis for his or her decision-making or behaviour.
• When given thirteen basic teachings from the Bible, only 1% of adult believers firmly embrace all thirteen as being biblical perspectives.
• Of Baptists (of all kinds) only 34% believe Satan is real; 57% believe that good works earn heaven; 45% do not believe that Jesus was sinless, and 34% do not believe the Bible is totally accurate.
• Only 32% of 'born-again' Christians believe in the existence of absolute moral truth.

Commenting on these findings, Professor Gary Burge of Wheaton College attributes such theological and biblical illiteracy to the following causes:

- The failure of the church to transmit what it believes to the next generation. One of the reasons for this is an over-emphasis on personal experience to the exclusion of serious Christian education.
- Many churches have abandoned serious Bible exposition and theological teaching. Exegesis is becoming a 'lost art' in the pulpit.
- Today there is a tremendous influence of non-biblical philosophies and worldviews on churchgoers.
- Christians have accepted and combined so many ideas from other worldviews and religions that they have created their own faith system. The average born-again, baptized, churchgoing person has embraced elements of Buddhism, Hinduism, Judaism, Islam, Mormonism, Scientology, Unitarianism and Christian Science — without any idea that he has just created his own faith.

It seems to me that those cheerleading for a Christianity devoid of propositional truth and centred on an experiential encounter with Christ should be pleased — they have achieved what they want. Scripture is basically ignored by the average believer, who instead measures his Christian life by how he feels and what experiences he has encountered. On the other hand, I am convinced that our Lord is not so pleased. He designed and commissioned his church to be the 'pillar and support of the truth' (1 Tim. 3:15), but the church is rapidly becoming a place without truth. David Wells informs us, 'Theology does not fare well in the culture because it is not believed; it does not fare well in the church because it is not wanted.'[12] He goes on to warn: 'A church that neither is interested in theology nor has the capacity to think theologically is a church that will be rapidly submerged beneath the wave of modernity [or swallowed up by its culture].'[13]

The roots of this weakened form of Christianity can be found long before the influence of postmodern philosophy. In a frequently quoted observation, Michael Saward, surveying the evangelical scene in the 1980s, could say:

> This is the disturbing legacy of the 1960s and 1970s. A generation brought up on guitars, choruses, and home group discussions. Educated, as one of them put it to me, not to use words with precision because the image is dominant, not the word. Equipped not to handle doctrine but rather to 'share'. A compassionate, caring generation, suspicious of definition and labels, uneasy at, and sometimes incapable of, being asked to wrestle with sustained didactic exposition of theology. Excellent when it comes to providing religious music, drama, and art. Not so good when asked to preach and teach the Faith.[14]

Where to from here?

As a result of these past and present influences, the church of Christ is facing an authority crisis. There has been a steady erosion of confidence in Scripture for several decades, cumulating in theological and/or practical elimination of the need for the Bible in our lives. After all, in a society infatuated with success — theological understanding, biblical knowledge, and even righteous living, are no match for fancy buildings, high-powered programs, the finest in entertainment and emotional experiences (no matter what the source). Very few churches grow numerically today because of solid teaching of the Word. That is because very few Christians today see the importance of the Word. To them the Bible is much like a musical concert — there to produce an experience, not to transform their lives. They see no vital connection between Scripture and life. To know God's truth is not essential to how they want to live their lives; therefore they have no desire or urgency to study the Bible. This leaves a vacuum that is being filled with mysticism, rituals, entertainment and fun, all in the name of Christ. Ultimately, however, like the sinkholes in Florida a few years ago, once the faith has been sucked dry spiritually there will eventually be an implosion. Without a timely recovery of the importance and sufficiency of the Word of God, such an implosion is imminent, although it is most likely to take the form of a slow degeneration rather than a sudden collapse. I believe we are witnessing such deterioration even at this moment, and yet few believers have noticed — another sign of our spiritual condition.

Our buildings are large; megachurches are prolific and multiplying; our programs are well-funded; the Christian entertainment industry is big business, and church attendance is still respectable, at least in America and in parts of Latin America and Africa. Outward appearance would reveal a robust evangelical community filled with ministry opportunities and overflowing with life.

But beneath the surface we detect serious concerns. Two generations of believers have, for the most part, been deprived of sound systematic teaching of the Word. An appetite for the superficial has been cultivated, and few crave solid food. Biblical discernment is a relic of a bygone era and is viewed with disdain by a people trained to cherish relativism. Such a situation cannot be long endured by God's church. Francis Schaeffer warned in the early 1970s:

> Once we begin to slip over into the other methodology — a failure to hold on to an absolute which can be known by the whole man, including what is logical and rational in him — historic Christianity is destroyed, even if it seems to keep going for a time. We may not know it, but when this occurs, the marks of death are upon it, and it will soon be one more museum piece.[15]

The Bible stands

One of my favourite Christian songs is 'The Bible Stands'. Although it is difficult to find in hymn books these days, its message has always encouraged my heart:

The Bible stands like a rock undaunted
'Mid the raging storms of time;
Its pages burn with the truth eternal,
And they glow with a light sublime.

The Bible stands tho' the hills may tumble;
It will firmly stand when the earth shall crumble;
I will plant my feet on its firm foundation,
For the Bible stands.

The Bible lays out its own claim to authority and power. Our familiarity with 2 Timothy 3:16-17 should not rob us of its force: 'All Scripture is inspired by God and profitable for teaching, for reproof, for correction, for training in righteousness; so that the man of God may be adequate, equipped for every good work.' Paul makes a radical assertion that the Scriptures are profitable to identify the true needs and issues in our lives, to correct us, to teach us how we should live and then train us in righteousness. When the Scriptures have finished their work we shall be found adequate and equipped for every good work. It is no wonder that Paul follows up this declaration of the Bible's power with a charge to preach the Word (2 Tim. 4:2) and to do so while there are still people wanting to hear and respond to its message (2 Tim. 4:3-4). Paul speaks of a window of opportunity that, with the help of hindsight, apparently opens and closes throughout history. We can observe an opening of the window, for example, during the times of the Reformation and the Evangelical Awakening. Now we can observe the window of opportunity for the Word, especially in the Western world, rapidly closing. We urgently need to proclaim God's truth while some are still willing to listen.

I believe the Word of God has the power to transform our lives, and lead us into godliness, and I do so, first and foremost, because it makes that claim. The typical evangelical would probably pro-nounce a hearty 'Amen' to the above statement — unless and until the claims of the Scripture run counter to the patterns of his life. When the authority of the Bible steps into the arena of his career, his personal habits, his psychological concepts, his finances, his marriage and family, his sports, or the way he deals with conflict, then, suddenly, the Holy Scripture is considered of little value and minimized, if not eliminated out of hand. After all, our friend reasons, what does the Bible have to say about such things? The answer: everything. Our friend retorts, 'It is an ancient book full of nice stories and good proverbs, suitable for worship services and funerals, but it has no reasonable bearing on everyday life, does it?' The answer: the Bible, through the power of the Holy Spirit, says that it can absolutely transform our lives — every aspect of them.

The Holy Spirit in Romans 12:2 indicates that everyone is born with a mind that is conformed to the world system. As a result we naturally think and act as one would expect those lacking an understanding of God to think and act. Upon conversion we become new creatures (2 Cor. 5:17), with new capacities to think and act in ways that please God (1 Cor. 2:14-16). But such transformation is not automatic. We carry with us into the Christian life the residue of our unregenerate, conformed state. It is for this reason that the New Testament calls on us to lay aside our former manner of living (Col. 3:5-9) and put on the characteristics of our born-from-above nature (Col. 3:10-17). But such a transition will successfully take place only as our minds are renewed (Col. 3:10). Paul commands us to 'be transformed by the renewing of your mind' (Rom. 12:2). Such renewal is possible only as the Word of God penetrates our minds and hearts.

The Scriptures, then, stand ready and able to expose and correct all our former conformity to the world system and its way of interacting with life. And, by the same token, they stand ready and able to teach us how to live and to train us in the right path. When Scripture is viewed in this way it becomes the indispensable power and wisdom of God to direct us in every area. The Word is not just adequate for church services, funerals and occasional pick-me-ups. It is adequate for everything, from child-rearing to job selection, to investments, to tragedies and loss. The Bible is every bit as at home in the workplace, in the hospital and on the basket-ball court as it is at a church service.

This becomes obvious when we observe that, immediately following the command to be transformed by the renewing of our minds, Paul launches into application relating to the most practical of everyday issues:

- Serving one another (Rom. 12:3-8)
- Dealing with people (Rom. 12:9-13)
- Handling difficulties and conflict (Rom. 12:14-21)
- Attitude and behaviour with regard to government (Rom. 13:1-7)
- Loving one another (Rom. 13:8-10)
- Moral behaviour (Rom. 13:11-14)
- Relating to those who embrace different opinions from our own (Rom. 14:1 – 15:6)

This represents just a sampling of the many areas in which the Scripture brings our thinking into conformity with God's. I would venture to say that the Bible speaks to every issue in our lives either directly or through principles.

The article referred to earlier dealing with biblical illiteracy ends with this sour prediction: 'Experts do not expect the trend toward biblical illiteracy in churches to change.'

But the prediction is followed up with wise exhortation: 'This does not alter, though, the responsibility of church leaders to do all they can do to reverse this dangerous trend ... we must try.'[16]

And, by God's grace, perhaps we will succeed.

8

Pastoring with Both Eyes Open

For the church of Christ to function as God intends, it is necessary that it should have the best in godly leadership. While it is true that Christ is the head of his church, the Lord nevertheless uses gifted and faithful men to equip and lead his people (Eph. 4:11-16). Therefore, it is important to give careful attention to the kind of men God wants to use to build his church.

With that in mind, we might first ask, 'What attracts men to church leadership, especially the pastorate?' It is rarely prestige, power or money (especially the latter). In most cases it is love — love for Christ, love for people and love for the Word of God. The typical Bible college or seminary student can hardly wait to leave the academic world and enter the ministry, where hungry and thirsty souls are awaiting his exegesis of the Word and his compassionate shepherding of their lives. With great enthusiasm and (as far as he can discern) pure motives, he enters his first pastorate with visions of changing hearts, building a powerful and God-honouring church and having an impact on the world for the cause of Christ. He steps into the arena of the church to be used by the Holy Spirit to help form the people of God into Christlikeness — and so he should. But few realize at the time that they will soon be waging great battles with the world, the flesh and the devil — battles more intense than anything they have experienced in the past.

Of course this is not altogether true. Having been well trained theologically, the newly minted pastor has an excellent understanding of the enemies that oppose the believer and the work of Christ. What our man does not usually comprehend at this stage in his ministry is the shape in which these enemies will actually be appearing. He expects to do battle with the devil; he does not expect the devil to show up in the form of well-respected and well-dressed church members. He expects to do battle with the world out there; he does not expect the world to have infiltrated the hearts and minds of his congregation. He expects to do battle against the flesh; he does not expect to see such raw manifestations of the flesh among those who claim the name of Christ — or at times within his own heart and life.

The expectations of the inexperienced pastor often crumble and transmute rapidly, and soon our man is disillusioned with the ministry, with the church, with his own life and too often with the Lord himself. Many drop away from the pastorate — and some should, for they are not gifted and spiritually mature enough to continue. Others drag on in the work for years, sometimes until retirement — and they shouldn't. Long ago their hearts were crushed, their passion lost and their love for ministry drained. But, as one such pastor told me in the first year of my ministry, 'What else can I do? I have no other marketable skills.' Far too often the result of this quagmire is that wounded and confused sheep are being led by wounded and confused shepherds. Many of these puzzled pastors lay down their swords and head for safer ground. Others, battle-scarred and weary, simply hope to survive, but the delight that drove them to the Lord's frontlines has long since dissipated. What remains is, at best, persistence and often little more than the necessity to make a living.

Something seems to be lacking in the preparation and expectations of pastors, and this absent component leaves them vulnerable to failure. It may be as simple as this — somewhere along the line pastors have missed the message that if they are to have fruitful and productive ministries they will need to pastor with both eyes open. They will need to have one eye focused on the Lord and the work before them, and the other eye scanning the horizon for the enemies.

I think Nehemiah understood this as he led the returning exiles in rebuilding the walls of Jerusalem. There was a great work to do but also an imposing and willing enemy. To concentrate on the work was his desire; he wanted to build, not fight — don't we all? But to naively ignore the enemy was to invite disaster. The people were afraid. They were not warriors; they were farmers, shepherds and carpenters and were out of their element on the battlefield. They had signed up to build great walls, not participate in power struggles. How do you build walls in such an environment? The same way you build churches — with both eyes open.

Seeing fear encroaching on his people, Nehemiah refused to give quarter. 'Do not be afraid of them,' he demanded; 'remember the LORD who is great and awesome, and fight .' (Nch. 4:14). There it is — they are to have one eye on the great and awesome Lord, the other on the enemy. Then theology was quickly worked out in methodology (as it always is). While half the people built, the other half stood guard (Neh. 4:15-16). And even those who worked did so with a weapon in one hand, or at least a sword girded at their side (Neh. 4:17-18). What Nehemiah understood was that there is no building without opposition, no victory for God without a show of force from the devil. But Nehemiah would not be distracted, or discouraged. Neither would he back down or compromise to keep the peace. He knew his mission — to build walls. He knew his God — he was great and awesome, and certainly not one to slink away from self-important warlords. Nehemiah had one eye fixated on his God and the task his God had given him, and he would not be moved. But he never allowed himself for a moment to forget that the enemy was still out there, ready to pounce, ready to destroy, ready to stop the work of God and rip apart the people of God that he loved. One eye on God, one eye on the enemy — this is how Nehemiah shepherded his people, and it is how church leaders must shepherd their people.

At this point I will part ways with our need to keep one eye on God. This fixation on God is undeniably crucial and foundational. Without it nothing of real value is ever accomplished for the Lord, but I will turn my attention to the enemy. Many a man entered the ministry excited about God and enthusiastic about the work, but was soon broken by the enemy. And at least part of the reason for that, I am convinced, is that they didn't expect to encounter an enemy, or at any rate not a serious one. When they do, they are disillusioned and totally unprepared for battle.

Let's draw some battle plans for two enemies that will show up regularly in every church and in every ministry. One, false teaching, threatens to infiltrate the church from many angles (we shall deal with this enemy second). The other, interpersonal conflict, comes from within — from church members who are at odds with their pastor and/or the church leadership. How these enemies are confronted will largely define the kind and quality of the ministries that will be developed.

Personal attacks and conflicts

I recently spoke to a group of pastors who were trying to address a problem. A number of the younger men were struggling with understanding the role of pastor as leader. They feared being called dictators and had become timid and passive. As a result, their ministries were weak, and the men themselves lacked confidence. In other words, they had been intimidated into abdicating their role as shepherds. Because of fear, uncertainty and doubt, they had chosen to run (or at least lie low) rather than fight. Perhaps most of them were kind and humble men who just wanted to lead the sheep gently. But while they were gazing at the beauties of the sunset, wolves were probably preparing an assault. And wolves are ruthless. It takes a rugged shepherd, one willing to sacrifice himself if need be, to do hand-to-hand battle with wolves. I am unconvinced that the majority of pastors today are prepared for such combat.

Books and articles dealing with the subject of pastors under attack are legion. Often these narratives are little more than sob stories and hand-holding. Most of them miss the fact that we pastors deserve much of the criticism that comes our way — and God knew this would be the case. Pastors are shepherds (by definition), but they are also sheep (by nature). We are shepherd-sheep or sheep-shepherds. Either way, we have been given an impossible task by the Chief Shepherd. We have been called to lead the flawed people of God when we ourselves are plagued with defects and blemishes. The best of us say the wrong things at times; we may be insensitive, distracted, too weak or too strong, prone to frustration, and the list goes on. We will offend people; we will wrong people; we will stumble — and we had better get used to it. One consolation is that our Lord knows what kinds of people he has placed at the helm of his church. This is not an excuse for sinfulness, but it is recognition that perfection will never be the mark of human shepherds. God is not surprised by this. He intends to build local churches through the labour of imperfect people, and that includes their pastors. Our Lord has designed things this way because the interaction and even the failings of God's people, when responded to biblically, produce maturity in the body.

Be this as it may, when theory becomes reality, when criticism abounds, when a power play is in full force, when the battle cry has been sounded, what is a pastor to do? Far too many falter at this crucial point. Somewhere along the line they have been led to believe that the pastor is to be a 'nice guy'. He is to be sweet and kind. He is to love people, not confront them, and never upset the members. He is to be a doormat, willingly accepting abuse, not a stronghold demanding biblical compliance. After all, the average pastor wants everyone to like him. He wants to please people.

Just where did we ever get this image of a pastor? Certainly not from Scripture. Paul, who gave us most of what we know about church and pastoral life, while always loving, was never one to back away from a fight when one was needed. When the

Corinthians challenged his apostolic authority he lovingly but firmly called them out (see 2 Corinthians). When Timothy was allowing some people to bully him, Paul told him not to let them get away with it (1 Tim. 4:12). Pastors are not given flocks so that they will have an admiration society, but so that they might lead their congregations in the ways of God. It is a hard lesson but a vital one — we cannot please everyone. We cannot be what everyone wants us to be. To make this our goal is to forsake our mission, which is to please Christ (2 Cor. 5:9). Until we understand this we shall never be the kind of pastors God wants us to be. As long as it is more important to us to be liked by people than to be approved by God, our ministry will be superfluous.

Somewhat over twenty years ago I read an article by Steve Brown entitled 'Developing a Christian Mean Streak'[1] which had a profound impact on my life. I had just gone through the most difficult time in my ministry — a time of gossip, slander and pure sinfulness on the part of a few, which led to division and spiritual harm for many. I had, along with most of our leaders, taken a strong stand against this divisive group. This action was not only the right thing to do but ultimately turned out well for our church. Still, I had nagging doubts about some of the difficult steps we had had to take, and I felt remorseful about things that I knew biblically and rationally had been handled correctly. Reading Brown's article reinforced what I knew to be true as he spoke of the devastation in churches brought about by weak leadership. I still recall that he developed an acrostic which spelled out 'WIMP' to describe his approach to pastoring. Brown's message was in essence that pastors need to lead boldly and not to be — well, wimps.

With apologies to Mr Brown, I would like to try my hand at an acrostic that I believe will greatly aid pastors as they face the inevitable attacks and challenges that will come. My acrostic is MEAN and, while this might at first sound over the top, I believe that application of the following principles will do much to enhance and guard pastoral ministry.

M — Mean business with the Word of God

Most conservative pastors spend hours every week studying the Word for sermons and various Bible studies. They sincerely believe that the Scriptures are inerrant, infallible and necessary for salvation and godly living. But when it comes to the real problems of life and resolving conflicts, they often leave the teachings of Scripture at the door. They believe in the inspiration of the Word, but not in its sufficiency. They believe in its principles, but not in its authority. They believe in its helpfulness, but not in its power. When an issue arises between members in the body, the truths of Scripture are treated as suggestions rather than mandates. The fact that God has provided through the Word everything we need in order to correct such issues seems to skip the minds of even godly pastors and leaders. Ideas based on psychology, common sense, or the latest self-help manual, take precedence over the clear and unchangeable teachings of God. The result is often a free-for-all of opinion, 'he said ...', 'she said ...' accusations, hurt feelings and division. All this is avoidable (unless there are serious doctrinal or moral issues at stake) by simply putting into play the principles the Lord has so graciously provided.

For example, below are some simple teachings in the Word designed to avoid and resolve conflicts that will inevitably raise their heads from time to time in any church. Every church leader needs to be well-versed in these truths:

1. The New Testament speaks of the great obligation and privilege of being a shepherd of God's flock (1 Peter 5:1-4; Acts 20:28). Elders are to aspire to the office (1 Tim. 3:1), not be forced into it. And they are to take the responsibilities of the office seriously (Heb. 13:17).

2. One of the areas in which elders guide the people of God is unity (1 Cor. 1:10; Phil. 2:1-2; 4:2-3). Even God's redeemed people do not naturally gravitate towards unity. They tend to find ways to bicker, get their feelings hurt and lash out at those who offend them in ways that cause

division. They need leaders who will teach and demonstrate by their example the biblical approach to conflict.

3. One of the ways in which unity in the body is broken is through words of gossip and slander. Our Lord anticipated this when he cautioned in Proverbs 10:18 that a fool spreads slander. Proverbs 16:28 and 17:9 are clear that slander separates close friends, yet Proverbs 18:17 shows that gossip loses most of its power when the other side of the story is sought and heard. Proverbs 20:19 goes so far as to command that we do not associate with gossips. These are wise and valuable truths that we must incorporate into the life of the church.

4. God knew that sins of various kinds would arise within the body and he gives instructions as to how they are to be handled. When gossip, slander, conflict, or evil is found among believers there are clear steps to be taken to deal with such things: Matthew 18:15-17 tells us to start with private confrontation, followed by small-group rebuke and then church discipline. But always keep in mind that the goal of this process is repentance (Luke 17:3) leading to forgiveness and ultimately reconciliation (Luke 17:4). We should constantly remember that we are a community of grace and thus a forgiving people. No one lives a perfect life, and when we fail each other we are to seek reconciliation on the basis of grace. Therefore we look for every opportunity to show kindness, tender-heartedness and forgiveness (Eph. 4:32), for the alternatives are anger, bitterness (Eph. 4:31) and division (Heb. 12:15).

5. The Lord also recognized that Satan's attacks would be especially levelled at the leadership of the church. If Satan can bring down an elder or plant seeds of doubt in people's minds, he can cause great harm in the body. Therefore the congregation must be taught the special instructions God has provided regarding elders. 1 Timothy 5:19 tells us not to receive an accusation against an elder except on the basis of

two or three witnesses. It is implied that these witnesses are willing to make public accusations, not orchestrate a whispering campaign.

These simple instructions, if followed, would greatly reduce the friction found in many churches and thus enhance the ministries of those churches. Yet many churches and their leaders behave as though God had never anticipated such problems and has nothing to offer in the way of a solution.

E — Enemies must not be allowed to define ministry

I use the word 'enemy' loosely since I believe that the vast majority of troublemakers in any church are what one author described as 'well-intentioned dragons'. That is, they do not see themselves as difficult people; they usually do not mean to be demanding, and they perceive themselves as being part of the solution, not part of the problem. What establishes them as enemies is not necessarily their intentions (which may be good), but their ignorance of, or refusal to submit themselves to, God's approach as described in the Word. Abandoning the biblical methodology, they apply an approach that is not sanctioned by God and has ensuing consequences. They become enemies, not so much of the pastor, but of the ways of God. If these people are prevented from controlling the church, but not corrected biblically, they will prove to be irritations within the body. They will gripe, complain and whisper in an attempt to win a few more to their cause. But, worse, if they are allowed to have their way, they will define the ministry of the local church and will do so in an unbiblical manner.

The problem is that most church leaders want to avoid conflict at all costs. They were not attracted to church leadership to 'do battle', but to help people. Little do they know that doing battle is a key ingredient in helping people and, when tough situations show up, they look for ways to sidestep trouble. Often inexperienced leaders are heard saying, 'Maybe it will blow over.' Yet, rather than blowing over, the problems become ingrained. Next comes the temptation to give in. Far too many churches are run by those who are willing to squeak the loudest and cause the biggest disruption. Of course such individuals, controlled by their flesh rather than by the Spirit, are the very last people who should be leading the church. The simple fact is that someone will lead in any local assembly. It should be the pastor and the appointed leaders, but if they are unwilling to fulfil their biblical job description someone else will step into the gap. Pastors who are fulfilling the role that God has given them do not run from the field of battle or hand the victory to the enemies.

A — Always remember who your Master is

The pastor who is working for the people rather than for the Master is at the whim of every voice in the congregation. While it is wise to listen to the thoughts of God's people, and in fact much of value is often gleaned thereby, only one voice must be obeyed. A church must not be modelled after the pattern of men's minds. God has already designed his church; it is not our task to rethink the church (as many are calling for today), but to unfold God's paradigm. I believe Ephesians 4:11-16 lays out the Lord's blueprint for his church perhaps better than any other place in Scripture. There we find that God has given to his church specially gifted men to equip the saints so that they might do the work of ministry, which in turn builds up the body of Christ. To dispose of this biblical model for a seeker-sensitive one, or an emergent one, or for the next fad to appear on the scene, or for the whims of a divisive group in the congregation, is to discard the voice of the Master.

Keep in mind that if you lined up 100 people who know you well and had them honestly evaluate your life as they see it, 100 people would be wrong in varying degrees. Only Christ knows who we are at the core of our being; only his evaluation is correct, and only what he thinks ultimately matters. Our task is to live to please him (2 Cor. 5:9), not our congregation, ourselves or the latest guru impressing Christians at the moment.

N — Never abandon the sheep to the wolves

Much as I appreciated Steve Brown's article, one thing grieved me. He said that he kept a resignation letter on file at all times and was willing to use it. While there is a time to resign from a ministry, far too many pastors give up too quickly. Most leave the field of battle during the heat of conflict, only to move to another church in which conflict will eventually rear its ugly head. It should never be forgotten that conflict is simply unavoidable; what matters is how it is handled. Nevertheless, to leave the sheep at the mercy of wolves, during the very heat of battle, simply does not speak well for the shepherd. Such a move may give temporary respite for the pastor, but it will not normally do anything for the local church except to allow the wrong people to gain control and inflict more harm. I have determined, by God's grace, that I will never desert the sheep when they need me most. If I were to leave my present ministry, it would be during a time of relative peace and spiritual prosperity, not when the wolves are nipping at the heels of the sheep.

A little 'MEAN' streak, as defined above, would go a long way towards creating more godly and biblical churches, and encourage the hearts of many a pastor and other church leaders in the process.

False teaching

Perhaps the most ignored prediction found in the New Testament is 2 Peter 2:1-3:

> But false prophets also arose among the people, just as there will also be false teachers among you, who will secretly introduce destructive heresies, even denying the Master who bought them, bringing swift destruction upon themselves. Many will follow their sensuality, and because of them the way of the truth will be maligned; and in their greed they will

exploit you with false words; their judgment from long ago is not idle, and their destruction is not asleep.

Peter clearly states that false teachers will be found within the church of Christ, and these impostors will secretly introduce heresies that will bring destruction to the lives of God's people. In the light of this fact Jude, in a parallel passage, calls for us to 'contend earnestly for the faith which was once for all handed down to the saints' (Jude 3). If Peter's warning is ignored, Jude's charge is equally discounted. Why? Why do most of God's people, including pastors, behave as though these texts were never written? This is especially problematic because these are not isolated concerns in the Scriptures. Not only did Jesus constantly confront false doctrine, but most of the New Testament epistles lean heavily towards exposing and correcting both false teaching and false living (Titus 1:9). Why should modern believers assume that these things are no longer important in our age?

No doubt the principal reason is that people today eschew the negative and gravitate towards the positive. The pendulum has swung from a time when people didn't feel as though they had gone to church unless they had their toes stepped on to a time when to step on people's toes might mean that they will switch churches. The most popular preacher of our day is a man who knows little theology, is not trained in the Scriptures, does not preach the gospel and ignores large portions of biblical truth (see chapter 4). Instead he smiles constantly, tickles his listeners' ears by telling them God wants them to have a wonderful and prosperous life and shuns any comment on sin or judgment. Yet every weekend over 40,000 people flock to his services and millions tune in via television. This pastor is merely reflective of our times — and he is successful. Preach a biblical message if you like, but if you want a successful ministry (in other words, crowds) you had better give the people what they want.

But what about God's warning of false teachers and his mandate to contend for the faith? The trendy pastor rides the waves of current fads and philosophy, but the faithful pastor anchors his ministry in the timeless truth of God's revelation. If our Lord has taken the trouble to warn us that wolves in the form of heretical teachers will attempt to ravish the sheep, we need to take him seriously and keep a constant watch for predators. If God has instructed us to contend earnestly for the faith, we had better strap on our armour and prepare for battle. If we love the people with whom the Lord has entrusted us, we will want to protect them from the danger of wandering from the truth.

Unfortunately there is much confusion in this area. Many, eager to maintain harmony among God's people, cannot reconcile contending for the faith with unity. Certainly Paul speaks of 'unity of the faith' as a mark of Christian maturity and something that should result from equipping the saints as we 'speak the truth in love' (Eph. 4:12-15). But the unity Paul commends is oneness built around 'the faith', which is a synonym for biblical truth. The body of Christ is to be taught God's truth, to stand on truth, to be united around truth and to dispense truth. Paul even describes the church as the 'pillar and support of the truth' (1 Tim. 3:15). It becomes obvious that the church has very little purpose if truth is not at the centre of all it does. Unity that is not centred in the truth is not unity of the faith, but mere uniformity. Where I live, we have one of the largest military cemeteries in the country. If you were to visit Camp Butler you would not find unity but the essence of uniformity — gravestones in perfect order, grass beautifully mowed, etc. But everyone there is dead. Uniformity is a good description of much of the church today — sociable, active, tolerant, compromising, and spiritually dead. Biblical unity, on the other hand, is a description of a vital faith wrapped around truth.

Since we are called to this kind of living, it is of the utmost importance that pastors devote themselves to both the careful teaching of the Word and the protection of God's people from error. Many pastors are dedicated to the study of Scripture. They painstakingly prepare their message and Bible studies using all diligence to make certain that they expound God's Word correctly. This is excellent and is where the majority of the pastor's energy should be expended. They must also be aware, however, that their people are constantly surrounded by a wide array of falsehood and half-truths in the name of Christ. There are few 'Christian' television programs worthy of the name; Christian radio is often a mixed bag; many Christian bookstores are a minefield where the very worst in Christian literature is sold, and the Internet is filled with every form of deception.

This is not to say that there cannot be honest disagreements among Christians over some areas of doctrine — not every hill is worth fighting to the death on. Nor am I saying that everything outside the four walls of one's particular church is dangerous — far from it. There has never been a time when more wonderful tools have been available to aid the serious Christian: computer programs, excellent commentaries and theological works, literature which shines the truth of God on the issues of life, and good Bible teaching from many sources. The problem is that few Christians have been taught to discern truth from error. Therefore, many well-intentioned believers swallow whatever is being promoted. For example, Michael W. Smith (a popular Christian singer who has often ministered at Billy Graham Crusades) heavily endorses the fictional work *The Shack,* saying that it will change one's relationship with God for ever. His endorsement alone may account for the sale of hundreds of thousands of copies of the novel. And he is right. *The Shack*, if taken seriously, may very well change your relationship with God — but not in a positive way. *The Shack* offers a view of God that blends Christianity with Eastern and New Age thought. The undiscerning Christian will not recognize this fact and could easily sink into a distorted understanding of the nature of God.

How does the concerned pastor deal with issues of this kind? First, *he is careful to keep before his people solid biblical teachings* — in the case quoted above, the person and nature of God. Yes, I know that many people would rather hear about self-image and how to prosper and succeed in life, but what they need to hear is about the greatness and majesty of God as rightly taught from the Word.

Secondly, I believe the concerned pastor *will keep both eyes open*, becoming aware early of potential trends, movements and books which might lead his people astray. He then educates himself, as necessary, so that he can be prepared in advance for potentially harmful matters that are likely to arise.

How can this be done, given the limited time most pastors have? First, pay attention to what the Christian media is pushing. What are the hottest books? What conferences are people attending? What quasi-Christian themes are being promoted in the secular arena? What new concepts are college students (including Bible college students) bringing home? What is making the rounds on the Internet? A few of these things will prove to need the attention of the pastor who wants to contend for the faith. For example, pastors might find, to their surprise and sorrow, that some of their people are buying what Oprah is selling at the moment. Recently, as was documented in chapter 3, she has thrown considerable influence behind the New Age movement (often called the 'new spirituality'). First, it was Rhonda Byrne's *The Secret*; next it was Eckhart Tolle's *A New Earth*. Both of these authors liberally quote Scripture — could any of your people be taken in?

Hopefully not. Maybe your flock can see through Oprah and New Age charlatans, but what about things closer to home? Take the emergent church movement (which has been discussed often throughout this book), for example. The emergent church is nothing more than a postmodern facelift of old liberalism — the same liberalism which theologically gutted the conservative denominations in the nineteenth and early twentieth centuries. But most twenty-first-century Christians have no concept of this, and when they read the winsome literature of emergent leaders they are attracted. This is especially true of impressionable college-age students. Yet, when I ask Christian leaders if they have read the authors that so influence their young people, I receive few positive responses. They seem to be unaware that Donald Miller's *Blue Like Jazz* is the most popular book on campus, as it offers a fresh view of the Christian life, at the same time using virtually no Scripture and distorting the biblical worldview. Nor have most pastors read anything by Brian McLaren, the recognized leader of the emergent movement. They might be aware of Rob Bell, if for no other reason than that his videos, called Noomas, are usually prominently displayed at most Christian bookstores, but they don't know what he teaches. It is hard to guard the sheep and contend for the faith if we don't know what the most prominent wolves are doing to wreak havoc among the flock.

Most of the important challenges to the faith today seem to centre around either the gospel (such as the New Perspective on Paul or Evangelicals and Catholics Together) or the Scriptures. Sometimes the Bible takes a direct hit, such as the Bible-code phenomenon or a destructive hermeneutical approach (such as Redemptive-movement hermeneutics). But more often the Bible is subtly undermined by the all-too-familiar approach of ignoring what it says and adding to it, thus twisting the Christian life into whatever form one pleases.

The last concern is so common that it is impossible to escape. The wise pastor teaches his people the authority and sufficiency of the Word. He further instructs them in how to take the ideas of men and women and run them through the grid of Scripture. This approach filters out the concepts that do not emerge from the Word, leaving only the pure truth. Unless pastors teach their people this type of discernment they are in serious danger of being 'tossed here and there by waves and carried about by every wind of doctrine' (Eph. 4:14).

Conclusion

Somewhere I picked up this little story about a mother who one Sunday morning went in to wake her son. As she told him it was time to get ready for church he replied, 'I'm not going.'

'Why not?' she asked.

'One, they don't like me; and two, I don't like them.'

His mother replied, 'I'll give you two good reasons why you should go to church: first, you're fifty-nine years old, and second, you're the pastor.'

It wouldn't surprise me if most pastors felt this way on occasion. A few years into the ministry, and many are asking, 'What have I let myself in for?' Their expectations of perpetually calm seas and constant spiritual victories have dissolved into turbulent waters and all-too-regular battles. This is not to say that the work of the pastor is not gloriously fulfilling and often abounding in fruit; it is to say that most accomplishments for the Lord's glory will be on the field of battle, not in the rose garden. The effective pastor must be prepared for this reality. Enemies, both within and without the church, will be his constant companions.

Surely there has never been a more challenging time to be a pastor. Pastors must learn to minister with both eyes open, as they fix their eyes on Jesus (Heb. 12:2), and yet remain aware of the enemies that oppose the Lord's work. Perhaps there is no better verse in Scripture for the man of God to memorize and believe than 1 Corinthians 15:58: 'Therefore, my beloved brethren, be steadfast, immovable, always abounding in the work of the Lord, knowing that your toil is not in vain in the Lord.'

Part III

EVANGELISM

9

Evangelism from the Point of Strength

There are few things that intimidate the people of God more than sharing their faith. When given the opportunity to communicate the 'hope that is in [us]' (1 Peter 3:15) concerning Jesus Christ, most of us break out in a cold sweat. We do so because we fear that we do not know the gospel well enough, that we will offend our audience, that we will be considered strange or stupid or, worse, 'a Bible-thumper'. We can overcome some of these fears by taking a good course in evangelism and by presenting the gospel as instructed in Scripture, with 'gentleness and reverence' (1 Peter 3:15) and with grace (Col. 4:6). Further, we can study and familiarize ourselves with some of the issues and common questions that unbelievers might raise. These efforts will help us to 'conduct [ourselves] with wisdom toward outsiders, making the most of the opportunity' (Col. 4:5).

Still, very few of us feel capable of adequately representing Jesus Christ on the unbeliever's own ground. After all, the gospel is truly a 'narrow' message which presents the unique truth of how sinners who are alienated from a holy God can be reconciled to him. It is only because of the sacrifice of the Son of God on the cross of Calvary that God's righteous wrath is appeased and ungodly enemies of our Lord are welcome to approach him by faith, and faith alone. It has always been an offensive message for, as Paul wrote, 'Jews ask for signs and Greeks search for wisdom;

but we preach Christ crucified, to Jews a stumbling block and to Gentiles foolishness' (1 Cor. 1:22-23). Therefore, the majority will not be receptive to the true gospel message, except 'those who are the called, both Jews and Greeks,' to whom it is 'Christ the power of God and the wisdom of God' (1 Cor. 1:24). That is, the gospel is the 'power of God for salvation to everyone who believes' (Rom. 1:16).

Presenting an 'unfoolish' gospel

If the content of the gospel deals with a holy God, a sinful humanity and the problem of man's alienation from the Lord, as well as God's provisions through Christ, and if most people will consider such a message foolishness, how then are we to spread the good news? The temptation in recent years, led by the seeker-sensitive movement, has been to remove the 'foolish' element of the gospel. That is, if the unregenerate person is not attracted to the message that centres on his need for forgiveness from sin and the righteousness of God, perhaps a slightly different message is needed. If we make a few changes, perhaps then the gospel would appear less foolish. For example, we could replace the idea that man is helpless, ungodly, a sinner, and even the enemy of God (Rom. 5:6-10), with the idea that he is lonely, needy, unhappy and unfulfilled. We could then package the gospel as a means whereby we could, through Christ, have these needs met.

No one questions that along with regeneration come numerous benefits. I do not believe that any true child of God would deny the privileges that are his (or hers) in Christ; but these benefits do not define the gospel, which deals with man's problem of alienation from God. By subtly redefining man's problem (i.e., sin and alienation from God) we can turn Christ's offer of forgiveness and righteousness into some sort of therapeutic catharsis. When Christ is turned into a means by which felt needs can be satisfied we have successfully stripped the gospel of its 'foolishness'. Who would not be receptive to such a message? After all, if anyone could simply place faith in Christ and have his problems vanish (or at least greatly diminish) what would be the drawback?

But such a message is not the gospel of Scripture; it is a tragic impersonation. In the sincere desire to see people come to Christ, many are guilty of offering a gospel that cannot save anyone. The great problem facing mankind is not therapeutic, but spiritual; it is not that we are lonely, but that we are alienated; it is not that we are unfulfilled, but that we are sinners; it is not that we have low self-esteem; it is that we have no esteem for Christ.

When we redefine man's real need we distort and misrepresent the gospel. As a result, many may pray a sort of 'sinner's prayer' to get certain 'goodies' but have no concept about redemption as taught in Scripture. Statistically such people will be counted as converts, but in reality they have been misled and have no knowledge of true salvation. As some have noted, we have through such means populated many churches today with tares who, sadly, think they are wheat.

Presenting the 'foolish' gospel

The point, for the purposes of this chapter, is that it is a vain endeavour, if not actually illicit, to try to make the gospel palatable for the unsaved. There will most likely be a greater response to this type of watered-down gospel message, but it is an unbiblical message and therefore is not the 'power of God unto salvation', and we are back to the difficult position we face as communicators of the gospel. If we change the gospel to make it more attractive we do not present the truth; if we present the foolish, offensive, true gospel of Scripture we risk alienating our audience. What is to be done?

It is abundantly clear in the New Testament that the apostles saw no options. A false gospel, no matter how sincere the motive, is still a false gospel and has no power to deal with the great problem of mankind. The only alternative was to proclaim the one true message given them by Christ. Theirs was not to attempt to improve on the foolish gospel but to proclaim it. They were to proclaim it clearly, graciously and lovingly, but they were not to modify it to fit anyone's theological agenda, philosophical leanings, or to draw in a bigger crowd. Such actions were clearly condemned (Gal. 1:6-9).

Having said this, it is no wonder that most believers feel at a disadvantage in their evangelistic witness. They are not free to alter the message to make it more winsome, so they must present the message knowing that it is considered foolish by most of those who hear. And while there is only one true gospel message to present, those to whom they speak can and do draw from a plethora of ideas, worldviews and religions. As a matter of fact, the average person today uses a cafeteria approach, piecing together concepts from a wide variety of resources to create his own unique view of life. Add to this the postmodern mind-set prevalent in the West which rejects absolute, universal truth and certainty, relishes relativism, despises theology and truth-claims and is content with paradoxes, and we have the makings of one of the most difficult kinds of environment in which to present the claims of Christ. No wonder the average Christian is intimidated.

A position of strength

Upon closer examination, however, things are not quite so gloomy for three reasons.

First, those who are convinced that the Bible is the written Word of God can have complete confidence in the truth it reveals. While the world is awash with an abundance of competing and contradictory theories and philosophies, God's truth is unique. In the Scriptures the Lord does not enter into a dialogue with us, seeking a playful give and take in which our thoughts are on a par with his. Rather, Scripture claims to have the final word on every subject that it addresses, and that includes the gospel. As we speak with people about their true need we can have every assurance that, no matter how feeble our evangelistic efforts may be, nevertheless what we have to give is absolute truth.

Secondly, our confidence rests not in our efforts, but ultimately in the power of God. While it is common in some circles to speak of certain people as 'soul-winners', the fact is that it is the Father who draws men to Christ (John 6:37,44); it is the Holy Spirit who reveals the glory of Christ to spiritually dead hearts (2 Cor. 3:10-16). No one comes to Christ unless the Lord makes the first move. If we are to take the Scriptures seriously then we know that men are dead in their sins (Eph. 2:1-3). Spiritually dead men cannot respond to the gospel message without the enabling power of God. Different theological positions might call this enabling by various names, but most recognize that, left to themselves without the energy of God, the unregenerate will stay unregenerate. This is good news for the evangelist. Bringing people to a saving knowledge of Christ is not within our power or job description. We need not be tempted to manipulate either the message or the hearers to bring about conversion. We are called to proclaim the good news; it is the Lord who takes the responsibility of bringing people to himself. This gives us the freedom to present the biblical gospel and let the Lord use it as he wishes for his own glory.

Finally, while the unredeemed may attempt to take the high ground of relativism, pluralism and toleration of the ideas of others, the believer knows a secret. Within the heart of every human being is implanted knowledge of the existence of God. Romans 1:18-23 makes abundantly clear that even the so-called atheist has encountered the evidence of God in the universe around him. The same is true of his conscience (Rom. 2:14), in which God has implanted moral knowledge with which everyone wrestles. It is not, Paul tells us, that people are unaware of the existence of God, but that they wilfully choose to ignore and suppress the knowledge which is abundantly clear. As long as they remain in this condition God's wrath will be upon them as he allows them to live out the consequences of their rebelliousness.

This is the knowledge that gives us a great advantage in evangelism: the unbeliever, deep in the recesses of his heart, knows that God exists and will somehow hold him to account for the way he lives. A war rages between how he wants to live (according to his fallen nature) and how he knows innately that he should live (as God has implanted this knowledge in his conscience). It is most likely that unbelievers will deny these facts to others and to themselves, but according to the New Testament they are true. As those firmly confident in the truth of the revealed Word, we can cling to what God has told us no matter what people say. So we have a window into people's hearts. They may appear self-assured in their belief system, but fundamentally they know that something is wrong. There is a hole in their proclaimed view of life that is ready-made to drive the gospel through. This hole, coupled with the truth of Scripture and the power of the Holy Spirit, enables us to approach people with the gospel from a position of strength. We need not be intimidated into failing to share the good news with those around us.

Jay Wegter, who teaches evangelism at The Master's College and at churches and seminars throughout the country, will in the next three chapters detail how we can effectively evangelize from a position of strength in our world today. I believe that what he has to say will be most helpful in our attempts to proclaim the excellences of Christ.

10

The Power of a Christian
Worldview in Evangelism

by Jay Wegter

On a punishing flight home from Nigeria to California, I prepared myself for the claustrophobic Frankfurt to San Francisco leg of the trip. After six hours had passed, I decided to stretch my stiff limbs and stand at the back of the Lufthansa plane. I noticed two well-groomed young men in their twenties engaged in lively conversation in German. My guess that their English was good was correct. One of the gentlemen turned out to be an Airbus pilot and the other an attorney in training.

After they discussed their American travel plans with me, I shared with them the nature of my missionary work in Africa. They were interested and polite. I prayed silently, 'Lord, give me the grace and boldness to share the gospel with these men.'

My opening was a bit unconventional: 'Gentlemen, it is likely that we will never see one another again. May I ask you both a religious question?' They agreed, though with a little hesitation in their body language. Here was my question: 'In your minds, what is the number one reason you don't base your entire life and destiny on God's Word, the Bible?' They back-pedalled a half step but offered an answer. The attorney said that the Bible was a book of moral wisdom like other books of moral advice but not the very Word of God.

I asked him how he had arrived at the conclusion that the Bible was merely literature and not of supernatural origin. He answered by saying that miracles don't take place in history or real life — so the miraculous things spoken of in Scripture must be mythical.

At that point I responded with additional questions: 'In your worldview is there such a thing as objective evil, and if yes, where does it come from? Can you trace evil to its original source? What is the human conscience and where does it come from?'

Both men were puzzled; neither made attempts to answer. I invited them to 'step into biblical worldview' for a moment. I began explaining to them that there is a very clear reason from Scripture as to why their lives are characterized by struggles of conscience. I mentioned that even their decision to be polite to me was an ethical decision of conscience. I went on to state that we have a conscience because our Creator has formed us in his image and that image includes a moral likeness.

The point I wanted to drive home was that their worldview had no explanation for one of the most pervasive human experiences — the operations of conscience. I raised a number of other ultimate questions as well: 'Where do we come from? Is God knowable? Why is there death and suffering? What happens when people die? Is there a universal standard of right and wrong?'

They appeared fascinated as I shared with them that the Bible answers every ultimate question with absolute certainty — and that these questions are exceedingly relevant to life. I told them that God's self-revelation in the Scriptures and in the Lord Jesus Christ reveals the very truths we need in order to know God, to know our destinies, to know our world and to know ourselves. I emphasized that what God has revealed could never have been found out by human investigation alone.

No doubt these men had never met a serious student of the Bible. I had dropped a very large boulder into the little mud-puddle of their erroneous worldview. As a result of our conversation, they faced a critical decision: either to consider seriously the truths of God's Word, or to continue to suppress the truth by attempting to explain it away. Our parting was friendly. They were grateful I had spoken with them and agreed that our visit had caused them to open up topics that they had assumed they could safely leave closed.

I am convinced that every true evangelical Christian wants to evangelize; he or she truly wants to reach our culture. But if we are to do so we must make sure we understand how our beliefs are distinct from the prevailing beliefs of our culture.

In this chapter we will examine the challenges to evangelism that we face in our culture. And then we will begin to think about how to present the gospel in the light of these challenges.

Current challenges to evangelism

Fragmented knowledge

The modern world tends to view biblical truth as a collection of religious ideas without any basis in fact. It is inclined to see biblical truth as a narrow subjective compartment divorced from physical reality. In fact, Christian truth is unified truth, consistent with reality and drawn from a single source, the Word of God.

On the other hand, secularist thinking insists that reality is nothing more than the physical universe. Reality is divorced from God. It has split the modern mind into two categories of knowledge: that which is real (physical matter) and that which is unreal (religious claims to truth). The Christian worldview corrects the deadly error of fragmented knowledge by emphasizing that biblical Christianity is an entire life view. Francis Schaeffer's comments are very helpful at this juncture:

> Christianity is not a series of truths in the plural, but rather truth spelled with a capital 'T'. It is Truth about total reality, not just about religious things. Biblical Christianity is Truth concerning total reality and the intellectual holding of that total Truth and then living in the light of that Truth.[1]

Because the Christian worldview is total truth, as Schaeffer states, only a biblical starting point provides the unity of all knowledge (the alternative is fragmentation). Thus the believer understands that all knowledge is unified in the Creator himself: 'For from Him and through Him and to Him are all things. To Him be the glory forever. Amen' (Rom. 11:36).

The world's fragmented view of knowledge is evidenced by the fact that unbelievers imagine that reality is larger than God.[2] For the natural man, God is only one component of reality. How radically different is the proclamation of Scripture — 'In the beginning God ...'! The Bible reveals God as Creator, Owner, Ruler and Upholder of reality. Since God made all things out of nothing, reality is God himself and his plan for the universe. This is our unified view of knowledge — all things exist for the Creator's glory. Views which deny that the creation exists for the glory of God will be left with a fragmented perception of knowledge. All things have been created by him and for him (Col. 1:16). God works all things after the counsel of his will (Eph. 1:11). The creation has no origin, purpose, or existence apart from the Creator.

Therefore, as believers, we affirm that *the Christian worldview lays the foundation for all thought* — it states that God's truth found in his Word forms a blueprint for every area of life and faith. This truth is vital if we are to share the gospel effectively. The reason is that we live in a culture which has lost the foundation, or framework, necessary for the gospel to make sense. As we shall see in our section on evangelism in the light of the challenges, engaging today's culture effectively involves laying the foundation of biblical creation as the framework for the gospel.

Sadly, much of evangelicalism has responded to the challenge of fragmented truth by accommodating the biblical message to human yearnings. God's blueprint for mankind is being cut to pieces so that seekers and church-goers can pick and choose the parts of God's plan that suit them. Consumerism characterizes much of today's religious climate. Appeals to receive salvation are often nothing more than thinly veiled offers of self-improvement: 'Religion will make your life better, your emotions more peaceful, and your marriage more fulfilling.' Remember we are dealing with a culture which has lost the underpinnings of reality — as a consequence postmodernists tend to view reality as flowing from self (the mind of man) and not from God.

Where secular thinking has crept into the church there has been a tendency to smooth the hard edges of the gospel (i.e. divine law, sin, eternal judgment, divine wrath). When the sharp angles of the gospel are rounded, you are going to get a different Jesus, a domesticated Jesus, who does not judge and discipline (or save). You will get a Jesus who is friend, but not Lord of the cosmos. You will get a Jesus who is mascot, but not majestic King. You will get worldly spiritualities with the sinner remaining his own god. Under that arrangement, the sinner may pick and choose the version of the god he can believe in (his litmus test is: 'Does this work for me?').

Regarding the allure of pragmatism and self-centred spiritualities, David Wells observes:

> They labor under the illusion that the God they make in the image of the self becomes more real as he more nearly comes to resemble the self, to accommodate its needs and desires. The truth is quite the opposite. It is ridiculous to assert that God could become more real by abandoning his own character in an effort to identify more completely with ours. And yet the illusion has proved compelling to a whole generation.[3]

Incorporating a biblical worldview into our evangelism can help us refute the error that self may remain enthroned amidst one's religious quest. Evangelism which incorporates a biblical worldview stresses that the sinner who believes and repents sees everything, all of life, in a whole new way — through the lens of the biblical, or Christian, worldview. The believer's new-found faith cannot be an appendage to all of his existing beliefs and commitments. In biblical salvation, everything in one's life is reordered under the lordship of Christ. Thus, effective evangelism is not merely adding information to someone's life; it is fundamentally a clash of worldviews, a thorough reorientation to another way of thinking.[4] God's total unified truth answers the problem of fragmented truth. This is good news for the Christian — the power of unified truth may be recovered through a commitment to a biblical worldview.

Moral relativism

A second challenge to evangelism is the moral relativism which accompanies postmodern thinking. Certain notions born of postmodern relativism are now so widely accepted that they are not even challenged or examined. For instance, 'There can't be one true religion to the exclusion of all others. Every person ought to have the freedom to decide right and wrong for himself.'

Not long ago my wife and I provided housing for a college student from Japan. One evening our conversation turned towards the truth of God's Word and the claims of Christ. Our student gave us a very postmodern response: 'My mother warned me not to spend time with Christians while in America because they think they have the truth.' Apparently, thinking one has the truth is the new bigotry in our increasingly postmodern age.

If you are involved in personal evangelism, you will face the challenge of sharing the gospel with folk whose relativism has left them pessimistic about the possibility of absolute truth. It is increasingly common to meet high-school and college students who cannot answer with certainty the most basic questions about their own existence. Like our foreign student, they equate open-mindedness with non-commitment to the truth. The college students I frequently evangelize typify the scope of the problem. Most are so steeped in postmodernism that they have given up trying to answer the following kinds of ultimate questions: 'Who made me? Who am I? What am I? What is a human being? Is there a moral standard outside myself? Why am I here? What is the nature of reality?'

After I addressed the largest Christian organization at Cal Poly Pomona, California, the director of student ministries confided in me:

> We are finding more and more in our evangelistic efforts that we are *talking past* unsaved students. In other words, when we try to share the gospel on campus, we are discovering that the foundations for understanding reality are absent. Postmodernism has given students a view of reality so steeped in relativism that God is inconsequential — outside of reality. In addition, the theory of evolution, like a corrosive acid, has been gradually eroding confidence in the reliability of the Bible.

This Christian leader's insightful assessment constitutes a wake-up call to every serious believer. It underscores the fact that our culture is rapidly departing from a Judaeo-Christian understanding of reality. Biblical Christianity is being marginalized as irrelevant; it is slowly being pushed to the edge of a precipice. The sign on the brink of this cliff reads, 'Warning: Christianity is implausible. Stand back! Dangerous intellectual drop-off.' In view of the Christian leader's comments it is easy to see why evangelism in our culture of relativism presents a unique challenge.

Anti-theistic ideas

Our culture's pervasive relativism is reflected in anti-theistic ideas and philosophies about reality. Our media-saturated age has supplied unbelievers with philosophic building blocks to wall off or shut out the gospel. In effect, unbelievers barricade themselves inside erroneous worldviews in order to lock out the gospel. They are like inmates who want to remain imprisoned by their false worldviews — they resemble prisoners who check the locks before bed. As if constructing towering walls of armament, the unbeliever has raised up fortresses of error which suggest that the gospel is implausible. The Word of God attributes the unbeliever's spiritual captivity to the false philosophies of the world (Col. 2:8).

One of the strategies in worldview evangelism is to tear down the 'fortresses' raised up against the knowledge of God. Only by confronting error will we establish the credibility of the gospel in a culture which finds the gospel incredible. Our evangelistic strategy involves *tearing down* the circles of fortification behind which the unbeliever hides. We must remember that the unbeliever has not chosen these strongholds of error as a result of doing careful research. The very opposite is the case. The unbeliever loves his imagined independence from God; he sets aside rationality and welcomes irrationality. In order to evade his accountability to God he chooses to erect arguments against the knowledge of God (2 Cor. 10:3-6).

The secularist media is more than happy to provide philosophies by which the unbeliever may insulate himself from the knowledge of God. Christian apologist Christopher Gornold-Smith notes the role the media plays in the growing acceptance of postmodernism:

Many people are buying into a postmodern worldview without even knowing what they are doing. Unconsciously, largely through the influence of the media, most of all through popular music and television, they are accepting a belief system remarkably different from the recent past.[5]

The non-biblical worldviews which constantly assault us in the media are readily accepted by unbelievers. Del Tackett explains why erroneous worldviews easily take people captive: 'Because we live in a selfish, fallen world, these ideas seductively appeal to the desires of the flesh...'[6] In other words, when the sinful appetites of men and women are allowed to set the standard for behaviour, as opposed to the Word of God, worldviews which permit the expression of sin will inevitably gain in popularity.

False philosophies

People attempt to hide from God behind their false philosophies. Believing in a universe governed by chance is a favourite among today's false philosophies. If the controlling principle in the universe were chance then naturally the gospel would appear incredible, unrealistic and implausible. In a purposeless universe the divine plan of salvation makes no sense. In a universe controlled by impersonal forces, there is no room for the perfect plan of our all-wise, loving, holy Creator who sent his Son into the world to die for Adam's helpless race. Scripture exposes the folly of such irrational thinking. God's Word sets forth the Creator-creature distinction as the very basis of meaning and rationality.[7]

It is a great encouragement to us in our evangelistic endeavours to know that every erroneous worldview is self-defeating. By this I mean that every false philosophy is filled with internal inconsistencies and contradictions. This is because only the biblical worldview corresponds to reality. All other attempts to explain or interpret reality will end in absurdity (Eph. 4:17-18). The Christian apologist can go forth with the confidence that the Bible alone explains human experience accurately. All false worldviews radically distort reality. As Peter Jones has aptly said:

> The Bible begins in Genesis 1:1 with a vast cosmological statement, 'In the beginning God created the heavens and the earth.' If one removes the foundational pedestal of [belief in the transcendent Creator, and] the Creator-creature distinction, then anything is possible. Once that is lost, all is lost.[8]

Evangelism in the light of the challenges

Let's turn our attention to evangelism in the light of the challenges of fragmented knowledge and postmodern thinking. The evangelistic strategy I am commending involves setting forth God and his plan for creation as ultimate reality. As such, a Christian worldview gives us the weapons necessary to challenge the unbeliever's faulty ultimate point of reference (his own assumed autonomy, or independence from God).

The students I train in apologetics often have a eureka-type moment when they realize for the first time that either God or man is the starting point for all knowledge. These two starting points are polar opposites. Either divine revelation or autonomous human reason must reign as the final authority — there can be no co-regency! The two sit in irreconcilable opposition to one another as authoritative starting points. When it comes to absolute truth, one is light; the other darkness.

Because this is God's world, the world works in God's way. Who God is and what he has said infallibly determines what is real, what is true, what is right and what is wrong. Everywhere the unbeliever turns he is confronted with God's created order. The non-believer attempts to explain away God's order but cannot do so successfully. This is God's world, not the world of the unbeliever's imaginings. The unbeliever's system for interpreting life does not correspond to reality.[9] Thus a Christian worldview is totally opposed to all thought forms and ideas which begin with self and which assume that man's reason can function independently of God.

In our gospel outreach we must maintain that it is God's character which determines what we are (the image of God), why we are here, what is required of us and where we are going. God's self-revelation is the only reliable starting point for all knowledge. If one's starting point is human reason apart from divine revelation, it is rebellion against God. To place reason ahead of revelation is to put oneself in a position not to know truth (Prov. 1:7).[10]

The Christian apologist may go forth with the confidence that *the only way to make sense of God, of the world, or of self is by means of a Christian worldview*. A Christian worldview forms a framework from which to view reality and make sense of the world. The biblical worldview is our starting point in evangelism; only the biblical worldview lays the foundational scheme for all thought — providing a fixed point of reference from which Christ, the living Word and Truth incarnate, is inseparable.[11]

While sharing the gospel with a neighbour of mine, I discovered that his professed belief in God was tantamount to belief in the divine self. His supposed knowledge of God came from within himself, not from the Scriptures. I asked him which he would trust if the Bible and his inner knowledge of God were in disagreement. He answered, 'I'd trust the god within every time.'

My experience with my neighbour instantly reminded me of a statement made by Pastor Tim Keller: 'The Western world is a new kind of mission field never faced before — it is ex-Christian — having been inoculated, it now has a distorted memory of Christianity as the age of prejudice.'[12]

My experience with my neighbour underscores the need for the biblical worldview as a starting point in evangelism. More and more Christians are seeing the need for evangelizing the lost at the level of worldview. Theologian D. A. Carson has over twenty-five years of experience in university missions. He notes why a fundamental clash in worldviews has become necessary:

> Knowledge has been privatized. Objective truth claims are viewed as coercive and an exercise in arrogance. The postmodern world is so totally relativized, one is no longer allowed to say that another's life view (or world view) is wrong. Moral judgments are out. If you make them, you will sound like a hypocrite.[13]

Carson's statement emphasizes why it is advantageous to lay the foundation of a Christian worldview in our evangelism. It is because Christianity's truth-claims cannot be successfully accommodated to erroneous worldviews. There are no sufficient contact points. Instead what is needed is a change in a person's whole frame of reference, or worldview. This is what worldview evangelism labours to achieve. Effective evangelism today increasingly involves a clash of worldviews — a fundamental conflict between methods of knowing.[14]

This thorough reorientation in thinking begins with the under-standing that ultimate reality is God and his plan for his creation. Every truth we present in our evangelism must be seen as deriving its meaning and authority from its relationship to the purpose and character of our all-wise Creator. This is our unified worldview — God gives every fact its meaning. He structures all reality — not just religious reality. Therefore, the only possible way to know a fact truthfully is to know its place in God's plan.[15]

The starting point

The doctrine of God and creation is the starting point for a unified view of reality. God as Creator of all — creating everything from nothing (creation *ex nihilo*) — has profound ramifications for man's responsibility to God. The doctrine of God as Creator establishes our accountability to God. Thus, worldview evangelism is strategic because it utilizes this big picture; it is God defining what he has made and defining the entire movement of history — creation, fall, redemption and restoration. The big picture is needed in order for people to make sense of Jesus and the gospel. The biblical worldview is the only vantage point high enough from which to view all reality in a unified fashion. This vantage point is vital in a culture which increasingly regards Christian truth-claims to be private preferences divorced from objective reality.

I am reminded of how evident relativism is among the young adults I evangelize. By the time high-school students reach their senior year, they are already thoroughly relativized in their think-ing. The experience at a secular college crystallizes what they already believe. Evangelism which incorporates worldview can help us penetrate the 'fortresses' of relativism.

How do we know?

Worldview evangelism seeks to bring a person's method of know-ing to the surface. Beneath every truth-claim resides one's method of knowing. In the disciplines of philosophy and theology, the term for 'method of knowing' is 'epistemology'. Every individual anchors his or her professed knowledge upon some epistemology (some authoritative source of knowing). One of the strategies in worldview evangelism is to bring to the surface a person's particular epistemology in order to reveal his or her innate hostility to the Creator and his claims. We bring the person's epistemology to the surface by raising ultimate questions, discussing them and then answering them from God's Word. For some, their epistemology is drawn from the methods and assumptions of modern science (with its core assumption of an impersonal universe); for others it is the views of their political party. For others it is humanist philosophy. For the Christian, epistemology is grounded in the infallible Word of Christ — the Bible. Christ has absolute authority in every area of knowledge. His lordship over all encompasses epistemology.

In our evangelistic encounters we must make sure that our conversations with unbelievers go beyond a debate over the meaning of facts. The reason for this is that we will not dislodge the unbeliever's erroneous view of himself, of God and of creation if we merely appeal to the meaning of certain facts and evidences (such as archaeology, textual criticism, fulfilled prophecy, or morality).[16] Something more is needed. The debate must go deeper — it must reach a person's epistemology.

Only by confronting the unbeliever's faulty view of God and himself will genuine conviction take place. We haven't really confronted the sinner's unbelief until we have taken him on at the point where he judges God and his infallible Word. When that takes place, the sinner is confronted with the inescapable truth of God (the truth that he already knows). He will be brought face to face with the Creator's claims upon him (Rom. 1:18-23).[17]

According to Romans 1:22, it is the unbeliever's epistemology (suppression of the knowledge of God and speculation) which makes him a fool. Concerning the contrast in epistemologies, believer and unbeliever stand on opposite sides of a bottomless chasm. On the biblical side, the Word of Christ is our authoritative epistemology. On the unbeliever's side, autonomous self is the trusted epistemology. A person's answers are either coming from the Word of God or they are coming from self. This chasm between epistemologies is like the Grand Canyon in Arizona — it is deep and unbridgeable. There can be no meaningful contact between the two sides without a clash between these two approaches to obtaining knowledge.

A clash of methods

The apostle Paul instigated a clash between epistemologies when he addressed his Gentile hearers on Mars Hill. Paul began with the biblical worldview. He started with the Creator and the Creator's relationship to the creation. The first thing Paul does when evangelizing the biblically illiterate is to lay a foundation, or framework, for the gospel. In his sermon in Acts 17:22-31 the apostle lays the foundation stones of a Christian worldview. In so doing, he sets up a collision between the pantheistic Greek worldview and the theism of the biblical worldview. Paul declares to his hearers that God is not who they imagine him to be. He is not a local deity served by human hands — he is not subservient to his creation. He is Creator, Owner, Ruler and Upholder of all that he has made.

In his address to the Athenians, Paul demonstrates the best way to establish God's authority and absolute claims upon his creatures — it is by means of the doctrine of God as Creator. This was Paul's approach: he was establishing biblical theism (the doctrine of God) in the presence of his Gentile listeners. Since he was dealing with people unfamiliar with the Old Testament, the apostle began his message with the doctrine of God and the Creator's relationship to his creation. Only then did he proceed to the gospel itself. We also are seeking to reach a culture that is increasingly biblically illiterate. We are striving to reach a culture that has lost its grasp of God as Creator, Upholder, Law-giver, Ruler and Judge. Without this foundational knowledge of God there is no framework or context for the gospel. And no context means we are talking past people when we try to share the gospel.

D. A. Carson highlights this important step in our Christian apologetics. He states that 'The doctrine of creation grounds our accountability to God.'[18] Satan's lie in Eden was a lie about God. It was a tacit rejection of the truth that all things are by him and for him. Modern sinners, by not acknowledging the Creator-creature distinction, are entering into the primal sin of our first parents. This is why the battle for origins is of vital importance — it is worth the fight. But it is a battle not won *primarily* by an appeal to specific facts and data. The reason is as follows: at the bottom of all debate over worldviews is *one's epistemology* and *one's claim to know*. The Christian apologist must ever be aware that the bottom line in all debate over worldviews is a question of epistemology.

This was my approach when talking with my German friends on the Lufthansa flight. I asked them questions which brought the core assumptions of their worldview to the surface so that those assumptions could be seen to be in stark contrast with the authoritative claims of Scripture. I posed questions such as, 'How does your worldview account for the existence of science, conscience, morality, objective evil, love, death, suffering and substantive hope?' I broke up this line of questioning into queries spaced out over the conversation. What proved to be almost shocking to them was that the Bible proclaimed the answers to these questions — answers which were perfectly coherent with reality. Having allowed them to share their worldview and its inability to account for reality, I was able to gain permission to share the biblical worldview with them, including the gospel of Jesus Christ.

Part of our task in worldview evangelism is to make people aware of the erroneous philosophies that they have assimilated. We need to remember that we are dealing with folk who have made a commitment to core assumptions that are unproven and unexamined. When evangelizing those influenced by postmodernism we must employ questions which are designed to bring a person's worldview to the surface so that this may be discussed.

Once a person owns his worldview (which he may recognize for the first time as he hears it from his own lips) there is a prime opportunity to present the gospel as the *exact opposite of what he believes*. It is this contrast between truth and error that is useful in bringing conviction by confronting the sinner with the claims of the Creator.

In the following chapter, you will see a series of simple questions that are designed to bring a person's worldview to the surface so that it may be discussed. These worldview questions are able to expose a person's epistemology so that an unbeliever might see how he opposes the infallible Word of God and its Author.

11

Sharing the Gospel in a Culture of Truth-Suppressors

by Jay Wegter

I want to share with you some of the questions that are designed to bring a person's worldview to the surface so that it can be discussed. Once a person 'owns' his erroneous worldview there is a prime opportunity to present the gospel as *the exact opposite of what he believes!* It is this antithesis that is useful in confronting the sinner with the claims of the Creator upon him.

The unbeliever needs to understand that he lives in God's world, and not the world of his own imaginings. The unbeliever's system does not correspond with reality because the unbeliever is suppressing the truth in unrighteousness (Rom. 1:18). Our goal in using questions is to find a point of tension between the unbeliever's illusory world and reality.[1] We want to show him that his problems stem from his claim to be autonomous from, or independent of, God.

The non-believer, whether he is aware of it or not, tries to explain away God's created order and God's role as Creator and Ruler. From conscience to ethics to aspirations to the need for love, everywhere the unbeliever looks, the image of God keeps 'popping up'. The unbeliever is confronted everywhere with God's order in the created world. He cannot explain things as they are — regardless of his presuppositions, the unbeliever has to live in

God's world.[2] Worldview questions can bring the unbeliever face to face with the fact that he lives in God's world.

Worldview questions

Worldview questions form a starting point for dialogue and a diagnostic for erroneous worldviews. The biblical events of creation, fall and redemption form a diagnostic test to examine every worldview.[3] There are four ultimate questions to test a person's worldview:

1. Where did we come from? (Who made you and me?)
2. Who are we? (What is the value and purpose of a human being?)
3. What has gone wrong with the world? (Why do evil, suffering, war, death, decay and injustice exist?)
4. What can we do to fix it? (If man is the cause of the problem, does man have the solution?)

After I allow the unbeliever an opportunity to answer the four worldview questions, I then ask an additional question: 'Has anyone ever shared the Christian worldview with you?' If the answer is negative I ask, 'May I?' Then I state, 'I want to invite you to step into the Christian worldview for a moment so that you might see how the Word of God answers each of the four worldview questions.'

Not only will this approach give you permission to share the gospel, it also opens the door to press the antithesis between the Word of God and erroneous worldviews. At this point I also ask, 'Wouldn't it be valuable to know where God's Word differs from your views?' Then I give the biblical answer to each of the four worldview questions.

1. Where did we come from? (Who made you and me?)

The Almighty Creator made the universe out of nothing. He upholds it; he has a perfect plan and purpose for it which he is executing with faithfulness, goodness and wisdom.

2. Who are we? (What is the value and purpose of a human being?)

We are created in God's image to know God. He made us in his likeness so that we might have fellowship with him. Our worth, dignity and purpose are bound up in the fact that we are created in the image of God. God has an absolute claim upon us and a perfect 'blueprint' for us.

3. What has gone wrong with the world?

When our first parents broke faith with God, sin entered as a destructive principle; it caused idolatry, death, suffering, ignorance, fear and separation from God. Sin is behind war, injustice, oppression and greed. God is righteous. He will someday punish all sin.

4. What can we do to fix it?

God has a perfect plan to restore man to his created purpose of knowing God, loving him, worshipping, obeying him and serving him. The only begotten Son of God came to earth 2,000 years ago to explain God to man and to lay down his life in crucifixion as a perfect sacrifice and substitute. Only by Christ's death is sin put away and forgiven. And only by Christ's death are men and women forgiven and restored to their created purpose to enjoy fellowship with God.

It can be devastating, even painful, for the non-believer to hear in quick succession the biblical answers to the four worldview questions. The biblical answer to these questions forces the unbeliever to deal with reality by exposing his false presuppositions.[4] Most unbelievers have never given serious thought to the major elements which make up their worldviews. It is important that we show patience and compassion. The unbeliever may be seeing his rebellion against God for the first time.

The only worldview that rings true to experience

The Christian worldview is the only 'key' that fits the lock of human experience. We already know from Scripture that the sinner's professed belief does not match his actual experience. Only in the Christian worldview does the data match experience. This is the exciting thing about worldview evangelism — you see correspondence going on between the Word of God and the unbeliever's inescapable sense of deity (i.e. the consciousness that God exists). The truth of the Bible resonates with the unbeliever's actual experience. The Word of God finds him out — discovers 'where he lives' in his mind. It apprehends the sinner and exposes his hiding places (John 3:19-21).

Let me give you an example. On a flight to the Midwest last spring I met Danny. He was a handsome football player and a recent graduate from a small private college in Iowa. He mentioned that he had majored in ecology. I asked Danny if he was a thoroughgoing evolutionist. He said that he was and that he sought to be consistent, interpreting all of life by means of evolutionary naturalism.

My next comment startled him: 'Danny, I don't think you really believe that evolution explains all of life.'

With a surprised look he said, 'What do you mean?'

I said, 'I don't think you believe that your thoughts are merely mental mutations — all of them determined by the properties of matter and without true significance — and that your thoughts are only there to get your genes into the next generation.' I added, 'Isn't it true that when you have a serious conversation with your girlfriend you believe that your ideas, opinions and convictions have lasting significance — that they matter in life?'

Danny immediately conceded the point. He agreed that chance and chaos cannot explain people, logic, morals and meaning. He thanked me for raising the topic of origins and offered the suggestion that much of his thinking was incomplete and made up of unexamined assumptions.

After my encounter with Danny, I reflected on the fact that we live in a culture that seems dead set upon thinking up new reasons why the gospel cannot be true. And, to make matters worse, these fallacious ideas about the gospel are then woven into popular culture, education and entertainment.

I was reminded after my conversation with Danny that many Christians would like to share their faith but find it daunting to do so. The apparent 'implausibility' of the gospel keeps the majority of believers mute in their witness. This is why I am convinced that worldview evangelism can give Christians the equipping they need. By providing a way to critique the unbeliever's worldview internally, worldview evangelism can embolden our witness. Just to know that the unbeliever cannot possibly live out his presuppositions is a source of confidence. I like to remind my evangelism students that the guilt in the unbeliever's conscience is just as real as the splinter in his hand.[5]

The value of antithesis

In Paul's apologetic he pressed the antithesis; he stressed the depth of the epistemological chasm between God's truth and his listeners' views. In our witness, we may proceed with the confidence that the Christian worldview answers every ultimate question. (Core questions, or ultimate questions, are: 'Where did we come from? Why are we here? What is a human? Is God knowable? Why is there death and suffering? What happens after death? What is man's destiny?' etc.).

We use a certain apologetic methodology in our witness. We *raise* and *answer* ultimate questions. Ultimate questions are reference points in a world adrift on a shoreless sea of relativism.

People have no certainty regarding their origin, purpose and destiny. Therefore they live in an atmosphere of fear, doubt, uncertainty, anxiety, moral relativism, spiritual darkness and foolish speculation. When Christ came to earth, he answered every ultimate question! He is the believer's certainty. I frequently tell my students that Christ is my philosophy of origins, purpose and destiny (Col. 2:8).

In 2006 on President's Day I took my family to see the Ronald Reagan Library. A number of characters dressed as America's founding fathers were giving speeches throughout the library grounds. I had my art supplies with me and began to sketch 'George Washington'. Members of the press were busy interviewing characters and library guests.

One reporter asked if I would answer her questions about free speech. After doing so, I asked if her views on free speech would allow me to make a statement. She agreed. My comment was as follows: 'God's authoritative mouthpiece is the Lord Jesus Christ. He has definitively told us what is true, what is real, what is right and what is wrong. If we refuse to listen to him, we sentence ourselves to drift on a shoreless sea of relativism.'

Her response amazed me. She said it was one of the most profound things she had ever heard. She then asked if I would sign a release for the video she had just recorded. I share this only to reiterate that most of the people I meet are grateful for a clear and compelling presentation of the gospel.

Irrational presuppositions

The assumption of human autonomy drives every erroneous worldview. Anti-theistic speculation is by no means a benign action; it draws down the wrath of God. Mental idolatry entertains false conceptions of God (Rom. 1:18). Romans chapter 1 tells us why the world is filled with erroneous worldviews. It is because the unbeliever wants to snuff out the light he has been given. The unbeliever loves his imagined independence from God so much that he prefers absurdity over the knowledge of God. Unbelievers reject the gospel not as a result of rational thought, but under the influence of non-rational factors. The ultimate commitments of their hearts to self and sin find expression in their suppression of the knowledge of God.

The unbeliever's worldview is made up of non-rational core assumptions which are designed to evade God's claims upon him. We need to be aware that fallen man has chosen a worldview made up of irrational presuppositions in an attempt to maintain his imagined independence from God. He has made a core commitment to a lie in order to keep his distance from God.

An inescapable sense of deity

The Christian apologist can go forth with the confidence that every unbeliever already knows certain inescapable things about God (he is Creator; he is good; he will judge all men). Christians have the confidence from Scripture that every unbeliever lives in an inescapable 'sea of divine revelation'. According to Psalm 19, every man is surrounded by the 'sermons' God has placed within the wonders of creation. Every natural man short-circuits the sermons God has placed in the creation and, in so doing, he demonstrates that he is a studious suppressor of the truth of God.

According to Romans 1:18-23, *there are certain attributes of God known to every human being.* We may therefore proceed in our evangelistic efforts with the biblical confidence that every natural man possesses the inescapable sense of deity described above. And we conduct our evangelistic efforts with the assurance that the Word of God perfectly corresponds with the moral truth which God has written on the conscience of every man. They are without excuse because God made the knowledge of himself evident *to them* and *in them* (Rom. 1:19-20).

As I mentioned earlier, when an unbeliever hears the Word of God, a work of correspondence takes place. The Word of God meets him at the point of his suppression. It shows the law of God written in his heart. It shines light on his defiled conscience. The voice of conscience says, 'I know that what I am hearing is true.'

When the natural man hears the Word of God he is confronted with the Creator he already knows.

The point of contact

Scripture gives us our point of contact between God's truth and the unbeliever. What is the point of contact with the sinner that is established by God in Scripture? We could summarize the answer by saying that the point of contact between God and his truth, on the one hand, and sinful man, on the other, is at *the point of man's rebellion*. The point of contact may be broken down further:

- It is God's claims upon his creatures (what he requires).
- It is man's sinful rebellion against God's laws (man's predicament as guilty).
- It is the image of God (it is man's intellectual war on the image of God — man's denial that he bears the image of his Creator).
- It is man's inescapable sense of deity (the fact that all men know God through the creation — Rom. 1:18-23).

The unbeliever's predicament

God makes himself known to the unbeliever by first setting forth the man's predicament. The unbeliever's suppression of the knowledge of God, his habitual breaking of God's law, his just condemnation and his legal guilt must all be stated. Men are not ready for the good news of the gospel until their consciences have been 'educated' concerning the seriousness of God's claims upon them. This is one of the most difficult tasks to accomplish in a postmodern culture.

In our efforts to persuade the non-believer of the seriousness of his dilemma, we must make certain that we aim at the heart as well as the mind and the conscience. When using apologetics with evangelism, there is always the temptation to measure success by the ability to 'win the argument'; however, our efforts at persuasion must be accompanied by compassion. And our compassion for the lost must be informed by the Bible's description of the unbeliever's predicament. Not only is the unbeliever enslaved to sin, self and Satan, but the unbeliever's hopes, dreams and every meaningful connection will turn to ashes on his deathbed when he passes out of this world without Christ. Therefore when opening up the sinner's predicament, I not only seek to do so with surgical precision, but also with the conviction that I am speaking with a person who is in dire need of Christ's sovereign mercy.

Meaning and purpose cannot exist apart from God

The sinner opposes himself when he argues as though he had a rational case. This is where the strength of the Christian worldview comes in — take the unbeliever back to his worldview and to his presuppositional starting point.[6] At that juncture, his system falls apart — man's existence, in order to be meaningful, cannot be grounded upon matter and motion, chaos and chance, speculation and absurdity. I explain to the unbeliever that his desire for a life of purpose is only possible if he has God, who is the source of all purpose.

Exploding the myth of neutrality

Christians and unbelievers have a world in common, a divine image in common, but not a worldview in common; therefore there can be no neutral ground.

Challenging assumptions of autonomy

Scripture exposes the unbeliever's faulty method of evaluating God's truth. Because men are ignorant of God as a result of sin, the point of contact cannot be in human reason or aspirations.[7] A biblical method of apologetics will have a biblical starting point —

the sinner's predicament. The Bible establishes a point of contact that exposes the sinner's faulty epistemology (which is part of his predicament). The unbeliever's epistemology (or method of knowing) operates upon the assumption that he is autonomous and not accountable to God. This core commitment to autonomous self drives the unbeliever's studious suppression of God's truth. In essence the unbeliever's worldview is constructed so as to invalidate God's claims upon him.

Though the non-believer poses as a neutral 'truth-seeker', he actually has an axe to grind. He secretly believes that God is not good; therefore he tells himself that he may determine reality and right and wrong for himself and live by the dictates of his own counsel.

He wants self to remain the ultimate reference point. Thus, his suppression of God's truth is not solely the resistance of the intellect to God's truth; it is the rebellion of the whole man. His erroneous worldview is not merely the product of a poor intellectual choice; it is the expression of what he believes and loves.[8] His method of knowing is guided by his ethical hostility to God. As Scripture says, '… the mind set on the flesh is hostile toward God; for it does not subject itself to the law of God, for it is not even able to do so' (Rom. 8:7).

We cannot allow the natural man's assumption that he himself is the ultimate reference point to remain unchallenged. There must be a 'head-on collision' between the Creator's claims and the false assumptions of the natural man. If we do not challenge his assumption that he can arrive at truth independently of God, he will interpret Christianity in naturalistic terms.[9] The concepts of 'faith', 'sin', 'salvation' and 'Jesus' will all be heard through the distorting filter of his worldview.

As long as the unbeliever clings to autonomy, he cancels out the ability to know truth. The unbeliever's frame of reference must be overturned. This can be done by taking him to what he already knows but seeks to suppress. He already knows that God is Creator, is good and will judge him someday. He already knows that the creation reveals the attributes of God. And he already knows that man is created in the image of God. Next, I show the unbeliever that his assumptions are 'on trial' in God's court. I want him to see his preference for a worldview that lets him determine reality instead of God. All the while I keep in mind that none of my answers will satisfy him until he repents and gives up his rebellion.

At this point I often return to variations of my four worldview questions: For example, 'Are morals really evolving? Where do morals come from? How can your limited perspective be authoritative if you cannot answer even one ultimate question with certainty?' By emphasizing the clash in worldviews, I am in effect 'smashing' the distorting filter of the unbeliever's false worldview and bringing him face to face with his Creator's claims upon him. A clash is essential if he is to stand red-handed before his Maker — a fugitive under God's moral government. Then I can begin to show him his need of the Saviour.

The sinner's real problem

There is great value in knowing the ethical condition of the unbeliever's mind. Romans 1:18-23 is the record of the universal corruption of human reason, and Romans chapter 1 stresses that the sinner's real problem is not intellectual, but moral. As an enemy of God, he denies his need of divine revelation in order to understand the world and man's place in it. A biblical apologetic emphasizes the antithesis that exists between the mind of the believer and that of the unbeliever.[10]

The antithesis is not merely one group of propositions contrary to another; it is about the whole life of a man. It is about the conflict of the ages between the kingdom of God and the kingdom of the Wicked One.[11] The antithesis between kingdoms centres upon the matter of the recognition of the lordship of Christ. I want the unbeliever to understand that the Word of God proclaims Christ as the truth incarnate. Reality is an absolute personality — the Lord Jesus Christ. Christ's lordship is over all truth, all knowledge, all history and all providence. Therefore, to reject

Christ's lordship is to reject his interpretation of the world and consequently it is to accept Satan's interpretation instead, by default (2 Cor. 4:4).

No neutral ground

Given the antithesis that exists between faith and unbelief, *there are no truth claims that are religiously neutral.*[12] There is no truth standard that is neutral. Believer and unbeliever live in antithetical realms of thought — they live in different universes of discourse. They have no common point of contact epistemologically. The believer and the unbeliever do not have interpretation in common.

Romans chapter 1 tells us that the unbeliever suppresses the knowledge of God. Central to this suppression is the denial that man is created in the image of God. The truth that God has made us in his image is inseparable from the Creator's rightful claims upon us as his creatures.

The believer and the unbeliever can have no common area of knowledge unless they agree between them on the nature of man (as the very image of God). Since they disagree on the nature of man, no such agreement exists. Thus, as a result of unbelief, there is an immense 'chasm' which separates these two antithetical realms of thought concerning man's nature. Therefore, the Scripture affirms an antithesis, rather than an agreement, on man's role as image-bearer. The well-prepared Christian apologist is armed with the truth that the unbeliever's denial of the knowledge of God is manifested by his denial of man's nature as the very image of God.[13]

Unbelief does not change the metaphysical reality that all men will never be anything but image-bearers of God. The unbeliever's claim to know is anything but neutral; it is informed by his ethical hostility to God. The antithesis is ethical in nature. Sinners know that they are covenant-breakers; they have broken God's law; they know that they suppress the truth; and they know that they should obey God.[14]

The Christian apologist needs to be 'epistemologically self-conscious'. In other words, to employ the biblical point of contact means that we are ever aware of the infinite chasm that separates believer from unbeliever in regard to their understanding of the truth. We must be able to demonstrate the antithesis between the systems of thought espoused by the believer and the unbeliever.

The ultimate source of authority

When presenting this apologetic argument, I begin by emphasizing that every worldview has an ultimate reference point, or source of authority (either God or self). I press home the truth that the Word of God condemns every worldview that denies that God is the ultimate source of authority. The Christian worldview stresses that reality is based upon God's plan for his creation. I then ask the unbeliever if that makes sense to him, and I ask him to explain how his worldview differs from the Word of God. This gives me the opportunity to set forth the truth as being the very opposite of what he claims to believe.

While evangelizing on the campus of Cal Arts University, I met a senior named Jason who was extremely well read in philosophy. His two companions appeared to take pride in their friend's ability to articulate his philosophic beliefs. As the conversation unfolded Jason began to issue challenges to the truth-claims I was presenting. Revealing his postmodern perspective, Jason commented, 'Why are you killing the conversation by making absolutist statements?' I back-pedalled for the moment and continued to affirm Christian truth.

Jason's next move, to the delight of his friends, was to mention that the evangelical college students he had dated were biblically illiterate. Jason had made two points: truth is relative, and Christians are shallow.

I stayed off Jason's territory and took the conversation back to the Word of God: 'Jason, has anyone ever explained to you what the Word of God says about your worldview?' His answer, 'No, they haven't', seemed both pleasant and curious. I opened the

Bible at Romans 1:18-23 and read the text with an explanation. Jason cocked his head slightly as he heard from Scripture that he was a truth-suppressor. As I explained the text to him his interest level soared. An appointment was calling him away, but it was clear that this glib philosopher was at a loss for words. I knew why. He had just heard his Creator's 'voice' in the Word of God. He had been 'apprehended' in the hiding place of his erroneous worldview.

Truth versus error

The apologist must not 'tone down' the confrontation between truth and error. By emphasizing the antithesis, the apologist guards against arguing with an unbeliever on the basis of his own worldview.[15] When we set aside the biblical point of contact in our evangelistic encounters, it permits the natural man's view of self to stand. Our point of contact is man's rebellion against God's claims upon him (as a creature created in the image of God). We must press the claims of God upon men without apology. Ask the natural man how his system differs from the Word of God. Listen to his objections, and then present him the *opposite* of what he claims to believe.

It can feel socially incorrect to engage in conversation which takes on the form of debate based on arguments. But the value of the biblical worldview in evangelism is that it can contrast, diagnose and expose unbiblical worldviews, all by using questions to gain permission.

Several weeks before writing this chapter I met a Christian brother at Starbucks for fellowship. As soon as we arrived, we ran into two unsaved gentlemen to whom we had witnessed in the past. After we had spent an hour with each, both expressed gratitude that we had asked to examine what they believed. Rather than interpreting our questions as invasive, they saw them as manifesting genuine care. During our conversations with them we also expressed concern for their souls and we pointed out where their views differed from Scripture. They individually thanked us repeatedly and said how much they anticipated the next meeting. How we need to remind ourselves that it is an act of incredible love, mercy and compassion to address the lostness and irrationality of the unbeliever!

What the unbeliever really lacks

The unbeliever does not have a legitimate reason why the Christian worldview is not true. The Christian apologist must reach a point in the conversation in which he challenges the sinner to take his faith out of himself and put it in God.[16]

The sinner may acknowledge that God is a magnificent 'category', but not the very meaning and rationality of the universe. When the sinner seeks to erase the Creator-creature existence, he is attacking his Creator, who is the only possible source to give meaning to existence. When training my students to share the gospel, I remind them frequently that it is not 'data' that the unbeliever lacks. What is lacking is moral and intellectual repentance. The non-believer has chosen an 'absurdity perspective' view of life in order to hold fast to imagined autonomy. I don't want my students to be surprised to find that the unbeliever does not want the gospel to make sense.

Appealing to the conscience of the unbeliever

The apologist is to appeal to the sense of deity that is in the very depth of the sinner's consciousness. Unbelievers frequently try to reduce the point of contact to a debate between personal opinions. Respond by asking, 'Where are your answers coming from?' Show the unbeliever what God says about his worldview. The Word of God functions as God's courtroom. Show him that his assumptions are on trial, not the revelation of Christ.[17] Your gospel appeals must go beyond horizontal arguments in order to reach the sense of deity etched in the sinner's conscience. Then God's verdict against sin begins to do its work in the conscience.

The apologist is to appeal to the sense of deity that is in the very depth of the sinner's consciousness. The natural man is always confronting the same God who now asks him to yield obedience to him,[18] and, as Romans 2:14-16 affirms, he is constantly haunted by the accusations of God's law which are written on his heart and fill the workings of his conscience.[19]

The things impossible with men are possible with God. Salvation is of the Lord. Only by God's Spirit can the sinner attain to a true knowledge of God and a true knowledge of himself as the image of God.[20] Only regeneration can reset the human intellect to bow before God's truth revealed in Christ.

12

Recovering the Neglected Elements of the Biblical Gospel

by Jay Wegter

There are only two philosophical approaches to absolute truth: the Word of God or self. These two philosophical approaches are irreconcilable and mutually exclusive. That is why antithesis is needed. Without a clash between these worldviews the sinner's imagined autonomous reason is not put on trial. In order for effective conviction of sin to take place, God's claims as Creator must be brought to bear on the sinner's conscience (John 16:8-11; Gal. 3:22).

When I teach evangelism, I frequently draw a map of the United States on the board. It is obvious that in order for a map to benefit navigation, our present position must be located on it. I am reminded of the humorous story of the Maine farmer who is asked by a motorist who has lost his way, 'Do you know how to get to Bangor?' The farmer answers, 'Sure do, but I wouldn't recommend trying to get there from here.' The point is that we have no other option in reaching our destination than beginning at our present location. We have to pinpoint our location if we are to navigate by the map. Yet this seems to be lost on some well-meaning believers who practise personal evangelism. The unbeliever must be clearly shown his exact 'location' in reference to Christ and the gospel.

The book of Romans is the most comprehensive treatise on salvation in the Bible. When teaching evangelism, I call the book of Romans God's 'map' to eternal life. When I share the gospel from Romans with a person who is unsaved, I take as much time as necessary to show the unbeliever his present 'position on the map'. I take him to the passages that deal with sin and unbelief. Before he can be moved to the part of the map which shows the way of redemption, the unbeliever must wholeheartedly agree that the divine 'navigation system' has located him in the portion of the map that deals with transgression and falling short of the glory of God (Rom. 3:23).

This seems obvious, but it is often bypassed. When God saves the sinner, he finds the lost person in a state of rebellion and pollution. That is where God locates him — that is the sinner's 'position on the map'. God's Word is the locator that uncovers the sinner's position and condition.

Only the biblical model of antithesis exemplified by the apostle Paul does justice to the mutually exclusive worldviews of God and self. The truth of the gospel cannot be successfully accommodated to the relativism characteristic of postmodernism. By the world's wisdom it is impossible to come to know God (1 Cor. 1:21). There can be no saving knowledge of God until the sinner fears God as he is revealed in Scripture (Prov. 1:7).

Greg Bahnsen, who is now with the Lord in glory, was a renowned public debater who specialized in the field of epistemology. He offered compelling reasons for the use of biblical antithesis: 'Without the ingredient of antithesis, Christianity is not simply anemic; it has altogether forfeited its challenge to all other worldviews.'[1]

Bahnsen shows us why antithesis is invaluable in showing the unbeliever the inconsistencies between his professed belief and his experience:

... if we are true to the antithetical nature of Christianity, we must engage in a presuppositional challenge to unbelievers to show them that in terms of their worldview they cannot make sense of logic, facts, meaning, value, ethics, or human significance.[2]

In our efforts to reach his understanding, it can be tempting to try to accommodate the gospel to the unbeliever's view of life. Bahnsen points out that 'we must openly challenge the apostate philosophic constructions of men by which they seek to suppress the truth about God, themselves, and the world'.[3]

Pressing the antithesis

Pressing the antithesis between God's truth and the lie plays a critical part in the conviction of sin. Antithesis is the light of God's eternal truth meeting the darkened understanding of man. God brings conviction of sin when this contrast between light and darkness is emphasized. Sinful man's heart-rebellion is manifested by cherished opinions that are utilized to suppress the knowledge of God. Therefore, Scripture calls for a collision between God's truth and the erroneous ideas held by darkened minds. This 'collision', or antithesis, is essential if the sinner is to experience conviction over his mental idolatry, or suppression of the knowledge of God.

As previously stated, by incorporating antithesis in evangelism we bring divine truth to bear on the conscience of the unbeliever. This is vital because the debate is not merely one opinion against another — it is God's indictment of the unbeliever's wilful ignorance of God. The non-believer is guilty in God's sight for what he does with the truth.[4] Antithesis brings that guilt to light.

If in our evangelism we avoid the step of antithesis we give the impression that the unbeliever is neutral towards the truth of God. If we treat the unbeliever as though he is neutral, it assumes that he needs only 'religious information' rather than conviction of sin. But by using antithesis we are following the example of the apostles and our Lord. Antithesis underscores the fact that truth is an ethical issue (John 3:19-21). Because antithesis shows the non-believer what he does with God's truth, it has the power to bring the appropriate weight of guilt upon the conscience.[5]

In the course of effective evangelism, we steer the conversation to a point at which there is an irreconcilable clash between sources of authority (God or self). The unbeliever's stubborn adherence to self as the final point of reference must be challenged, or he will continue to spew out objections to the gospel. Remember, our witness is aimed at repentance. The Christian apologist must always be aware that sinners will not be satisfied with the answers we give until they give up their rebellion against God.[6]

The unbeliever's rebellion against God is manifested by the fact that self is his non-negotiable starting point and controlling presupposition. Once we understand that the natural man has no fixed point of reference outside of himself, we can employ antithesis by contrasting the sinner's point of reference to the authority of God's Word. Without antithesis, the sinner's controlling presupposition remains uncontested. What the unbeliever thinks about himself and what God says about him must be put into bold contrast. This is because the sinner still imagines that the answer to his spiritual dilemma remains in his own hands. We must challenge his ultimate reference point so that his opposition to God is brought to light.

Without this humbling convicting stage, our evangelistic efforts are like painting over the barnacles on the rotten hull of a ship. The polluted condition of the heart must be revealed before the remedy of the gospel will ever be embraced. By making use of antithesis in our witness, we are able to show that the assumptions of the unbeliever are on trial in God's court. To put it bluntly, the Creator never leaves the sinner's assumed autonomy intact. Throughout Scripture God declares that his Word is a fixed, immovable point of reference that stands in antithesis to self. Self-reliance, the world's approach to knowledge, is condemned by God as folly (Prov. 1:7; 3:5; Jer. 17:5).

The unbeliever's problem is not that he has no idea who God is. His problem is that he does not *like* who God is; therefore he rejects divine wisdom. This is the cause of the non-believer's rash speculations about reality. The sinner's intellectual problem is produced by his moral condition (as a spiritually dead individual in need of regeneration).[7] The faithful Christian apologist is mindful that, to a large extent, we take to the unbeliever what he already knows but seeks to suppress — the knowledge of God (Rom 1:19-20).

Several years ago my ministry partner in university missions invited Anthony, an unsaved college friend, to my home. The moment Anthony walked through the door I could tell that his conscience was troubling him. His Roman Catholic training was unable to provide any liberty for his conscience. He had recently begun reading the Bible and had noticed the dichotomy between the Word of God and the empty word of man found in so much religious ceremony.

Anthony ventured to ask me a question from his readings in the Gospel of John: 'What does it mean, "Behold, the Lamb of God who takes away the sin of the world!"?' (John 1:29). I sensed that he was already under the Spirit's conviction. As I opened up the Scriptures, giving a reasoned explanation as to why God had commanded animal sacrifice in the Old Testament, the young man began to perspire profusely. I was sharing with him why the character of God requires justice. But what surprised me most was his reply when I explained the all-sufficient satisfaction wrought by Christ's sacrifice as 'God's Lamb'.

In a troubled voice Anthony said, 'I am so afraid right now, my heart is racing.' My answer to his tremulous state was: 'Friend, God is sinking your little "ship" of religious hope — the Lord is sending cannon fire above the water line and torpedoes below the water line… It is sinking — it cannot save you from sin and judgment — it is filled with holes above and below the water line. I urge you to abandon ship and put all your trust in Christ alone. He will receive you, forgive you and save you.'

Though cast as a metaphor, my counsel to Anthony was pure antithesis. It was a contrast between his present false hope based on religious ritual and the true hope found in Christ alone. To my joy, Anthony gave his life to Christ later that week. As I write, he is a growing, useful Christian who is scheduled to take his first short-term mission trip this summer.

Commonly neglected elements in today's evangelism

The church today is afflicted by a gospel which requires no *repentance*. The words of Welsh pastor Howell Harris are even more true today than they were 200 years ago: 'Churches are filled with folks who have a détente with sin; they are at ease under its dominion. They won't study the fruits of faith or make their election and calling sure, but turn the grace of God into licentiousness.'[8]

Harris's point is well taken — we have forgotten the necessity of *deep conviction of sin*. God's grace is free, but there are conditions attached to its bestowal which are set by the Holy Spirit. The Spirit prepares the sinner for grace by means of conviction (John 16:8-11). The burden of sin and wrath on the conscience is a function of divine grace because Christ's merit is known only to the poor soul in deep distress. Small conviction of sin will yield only slight views of Christ's blood and merits.

There is a necessary *desperation* which must accompany true conviction of sin. It is only the destitute sinner who falls at the feet of Christ. Only those who have been smitten with the death-wound of impending damnation flee to the Saviour. Only those stripped of all self-righteousness cry to Christ for mercy. The unsaved 'religious' man has yet to receive a death-blow from the law of God. The law has never been manifested to him in its spirituality (Rom. 7:14); in other words, he has never been thoroughly slain by the law. If he had been, he would be dead to the law as a source of life. He would understand that he must find spiritual life in another, and not in law-keeping (Gal. 2:19).

As a consequence of being still alive to the law, the idol of self is set up in the heart over against Christ in his offices of Priest and

King. The false professor (i.e. nominal Christian) feels that he is a good Christian *before* he is thoroughly condemned by the law. Only when the law slays him will he be made to feel his utter need of faith in order to lay hold of Christ's imputed righteousness.[9]

Only the Spirit's convicting power can make an end of self-help. Thomas Wilcox says:

Nature can't stand being stripped of all righteousness. Nature would rather despair, would rather choose Judas' noose, than go to Christ on His terms. 'Be merciful to me the sinner' is the hardest prayer in the world. To confess Christ from the heart is above the power of flesh and blood.[10]

I find myself in agreement with Wilcox — namely, that so much profession of Christianity today is merely an 'accommodation', or lowering of the market, to what the flesh is capable of performing. Profession without conversion is a form of religion in which men have never actually parted with self-righteousness. As a result, those who have made such a profession trust in their own merits and consequently are strangers to the blood of Christ.

The unregenerate person lies in a deep spiritual slumber of apathy. All his false hopes must be dashed, or he will never flee to Christ. Those who have made a false profession of faith are more naked, wretched and poor than they can possibly imagine. They have not seen their own moral bankruptcy and spiritual ruin. They seem ignorant of the fact that God only pities, forgives and receives those who are poor in spirit, self-condemned, broken-hearted and sincere. Apart from the Spirit's work no man can prepare himself in this way. It is the Spirit's convicting work to harrow the heart until it is 'mortally wounded' by the law. In the words of Howell Harris:

Now no man ever came into liberty without feeling himself in bondage: no man ever truly believed without finding it, through an evil heart of unbelief, the hardest thing in the world; nor did any ever deny themselves and take up the cross without perceiving hell, darkness, and wrath, everywhere pursuing them, until taken into Christ, the only Refuge.[11]

God's way is radically different from the self-salvation inherent in modern evangelistic methods. God comes down and scatters every stick, stone and pile of mortar that the sinner has built in the interests of personal merit. When the Spirit does his convicting work, he does not leave one stone upon another. He is a jealous God and will have no partner in the work of salvation.

When the quickening power of God's Spirit has passed upon a man's conscience, he is brought to see himself to be morally and spiritually bankrupt. This inward sight of self cuts him off sooner or later from any hope of being saved by law-keeping. In many cases the work may begin in a way that is scarcely perceptible, but be sure of this: the Lord will bring down the hearts of all his people with labour; he will convince them of their lost state before him and cast them as ruined wretches into the dust of death — without hope, strength, wisdom, help, or righteousness, except that which is given to them as a free gift of distinguishing grace (Rom. 5:6-11). Our problem today is that we want conversions without conviction. We urge sinners to take Christ as Saviour before they have undergone any trauma of soul over their sins.

This work of grace in the conscience, pulling down all of man's false refuges, stripping him of every lying hope and thrusting him down into self-abasement and self-abhorrence, is indispensable to a true reception of Christ. No matter how informed his judgment may be, he will never receive Christ spiritually into his heart and affections until he has been broken in his soul by the hand of God and acknowledges himself to be a ruined wretch.[12]

We need to recover the gospel essentials

The biblical gospel must include the character of God and the character of the sinner. The true gospel contains the following essentials:

1. Who has the sinner offended?
2. How has the sinner offended God?
3. What are the consequences of offending God?
4. What are sinners to be saved from?
5. What has God done about the sinner's dilemma?
6. How are sinners to be saved from ruin?

Who has the sinner offended?

Our gospel message must have at its core the glory, majesty and exaltation of God — he is the offended power. Without the knowledge of the God whom he has offended, the sinner will not see himself in opposition to God.[13] The gospel is about God, whom the sinner has offended, about the Creator's moral majesty and righteous justice. God cannot be made to fit the sinner's instincts, radical miscalculations and subjective ideas of deity. All conviction of sin and remorse for sin begins with the character of God as he is revealed in Scripture.

In your witness, start with God as Creator — begin with who God is in relation to all else (i.e. his absolute claims upon his creatures). As Ken Ham says:

> Don't assume the culture knows anything about God. Don't try to lead someone to Christ who doesn't understand God's character. False evangelism tries to attract by focusing on divine love to the exclusion of God's holiness, sovereignty and righteous justice.

How has the sinner offended God?

Man must experience a degree of devastation about personal sin. The modern gospel circumvents this step. There must be an awakening in the individual as to the fact that all sin is against God, against his holy character. There is no repentance until the sinner says the same thing about his sin that God does. Sin makes him an enemy of God (Rom. 3:23; 5:10).

Jesus took the rich young ruler back to the law of God (Luke 18:18-23). The sinner must be shown how he has specifically offended God. The cross cannot be made personal without making the sinner's depravity personal (that is, the transgressor must be shown that who he is and what he personally has done has offended God). The preaching of the law is the tool for identifying sin (Rom. 3:20; 5:20).

In our culture, people hear the gospel through a grid of self-improvement. They assume that the gospel is about them, about their self-therapy, not about God, who is glorified in judging sin at the cross and thereby redeeming and reconciling the sinner.

What are the consequences of offending God?

The law stops every mouth so that all may become guilty before God (Rom. 3:19). Man's 'uneducated conscience' cannot be trusted to assess the seriousness of sin and its verdict of death and separation from God. Only through the proclamation of the character of God and the immutability of his law will sinners conclude that they are lawbreakers in God's sight who deserve eternal condemnation (1 John 3:4).

The law is the identifier of sin — without the law, how does a person know what to repent of? Modern evangelism ignores God's law. As a consequence, the modern gospel is emptied of the gospel essentials of sin, hell, conviction and repentance. God has borne witness to man's moral and spiritual condition. God is just and fair to shut impenitent sinners out of the enjoyment of his glory for ever (Matt. 10:28). Sinners who reject God's authority, who do not fear God or believe God, are liable to death and judgment (Matt. 12:36). They will experience God's verdict — the separation of their souls from God for ever in eternal punishment (Rom. 6:23). Sinners make a wager, or gamble, that God will not judge them eternally for their sins (Ps. 10:13).

What are sinners to be saved from?

Sinners must be told that they need to be saved not only from the consequences of sin (death and separation from God in hell), but also from sin itself. Salvation is not merely deliverance from the *penalty* of sin, but also deliverance from the *dominion* of sin. This is absolutely vital — it is a truth inherent in true repentance (Luke 13:5; 24:47). The individual who truly repents wants to be freed from the tyranny of sin. Jesus felt a love for the rich young ruler, then told him what he must be saved from — covetousness (Luke 18:22-23). Sinners need to know that they must be saved from the wrath of God, which will justly come upon all who do not believe the gospel and repent of sin (Rom. 2:1-10). The fact that God will someday lay bare every heart is stated in a gospel context (Rom. 2:16).

What has God done about the sinner's dilemma?

Without knowledge of God, whom the sinner has offended, and without knowledge of God's law, which the sinner has trampled, there will be no grasp of what God has done to save. Grace makes sense only to those who see themselves as condemned law-breakers. The good news of the gospel is that there is an almighty, living God who is Creator. He has taken on flesh and dwelled with mankind. Christ the God-man died for our sins according to the Scriptures. By his substitutionary death, he fulfilled the long-awaited promise of a perfect redemption. He established the new covenant in his blood (Matt. 26:28; 1 Cor. 11:25).

The atonement Christ has made exalts divine justice. Because of the cross, God is glorified in extending full and free forgiveness to believing sinners. By his resurrection from the dead, Jesus conquered sin, Satan and death. His resurrection is proof that the Father has accepted the Son's sacrifice on behalf of all who will believe. God is ready to receive even the worst sinner who believes and repents — because Christ has provided the all-sufficient sacrifice for sin.

How are sinners to be saved from ruin?

The promise of eternal life is offered to all who believe and repent: 'Turn from your sins and follow Christ — take hold of eternal life!' God is focusing his mighty power in the gospel — in saving sinners (Rom. 1:16-17). The good news of the gospel is that men and women may have certainty about forgiveness of personal sin and may have eternal life through a personal relationship with Jesus Christ (John 3:36; 5:24-25; 10:27-29).

We are to proclaim the gospel with authority, as heralds of the good news: 'God desires you to be saved — he even commands you to come to him and be forgiven, to be reconciled to him on the basis of what he has done in Christ Jesus (Isa. 55:3-7). You need not remain an enemy estranged from him — he has promised to receive all those who come to him by faith in his Son (John 1:12-13; 6:37; Acts 17:30-31). Christ is calling sinners to repentance and faith. These are twin graces that will be present in the regenerate person. Repentance and faith enable the sinner to flee to Christ and take hold of him as Saviour (Phil. 1:29; Eph. 2:8-10).'

A false diagnosis

The problem with modern evangelism is its false diagnosis of the sinner's dilemma. Without a correct diagnosis of the sinner's condition in God's sight, men will resent and resist the gospel. Apart from the Holy Spirit using the law, men tend to hide themselves from the exposure and judgment of their sin. No man welcomes the cure provided by the cross until he sees that his 'sin disease' is eternally fatal. A man does not understand the gospel if he has no understanding of divine law. The law is the means of showing the sinner that God is 'Moral Governor' of the universe. The law now has both a preceptive role (commandments) and an evangelical role (conviction of sin). Its evangelical role is to make sin exceedingly sinful (Rom. 7:13). We are therefore to preach the law in a manner that is lethal to every hope that the sinner entertains of contributing to his own salvation. The law in the hands of the Spirit removes the sinner's false hope in good works as being able to save him.

Early Puritans such as Robert Bolton (1606–1654) recognized the danger of 'short-cutting' the gospel by offering free grace *before* the conscience was afflicted by the law.[14] The Puritans regarded the moral law as a codified copy of the divine nature (God's holiness in transcript), an unchanging expression of the holy majesty of God's person. Since God's moral government is founded upon his law, the ineffable principle of moral cause and effect reveals God's righteous character. The Puritans recognized that the moral law was the standard by which God would judge the world and condemn the ungodly, but they also perceived its saving use as it utterly destroyed men's self-confidence, revealed their guilt and pollution and drove them to Christ.[15]

Under the new covenant, the evangelical role of the law is summarized in Galatians 2 – 3. In these chapters the law places the entire human race in custody awaiting judgment; thus the moral law of God operates like a bulldozer that scrapes human merit off the face of the earth.

In fulfilling its evangelical role, the law is pictured in the book of Galatians as a prosecutor, an executioner, a jailor, a tutor, and as one who pronounces a curse; thus the law prepares the sinner for the gospel by destroying all his false hopes and by exposing his condemned condition before God (Rom. 10:4).

A suggested procedure for using the law in apologetics and evangelism

Establish the very concept of moral law

Ask key questions to make sure the person with whom you are sharing understands that God governs by means of his law. Note how our culture separates the person of God from the moral law of God. In your evangelism, strive to join the person of God to his unchanging law. God's law is an expression of his loving care of us. To break his laws is to sin against God's character and it is to sin against love, which God's laws are meant to safeguard.

Establish that moral law is a direct reflection of God's unchanging moral character

It is impossible to love God without submitting to and valuing his commands as the expression of his righteousness (Deut. 30:19-20). The Leviticus formula is: 'I am the LORD; therefore...' God's standard never evolves, because the Lawgiver never changes. His moral law for man reflects the immutable character of his righteousness and holiness. It is a standard that is eternally binding upon all civilizations.[16]

Establish the existence of God's moral government

Moral cause and effect are administered by God (note Deut. 10; 11; 13; 27; 28). By obedience to God's commands, we manifest that we are God's possession and that we are willingly subject to his moral government. Paul preached the gospel against the backdrop of the coming judgment of God's moral government (see Acts 17:30-31; 24:15,16; Rom. 2:16). To reverence God and his moral authority is to understand that sin pays the wages, or salary, of death and separation (Rom. 6:23).

Remember that every false worldview has its own erroneous counterpart to the biblical doctrines of sin, moral guilt, atonement and salvation. In a rudimentary fashion, God's law is written on the conscience of every man (Rom. 2:15). We can tap into this innate knowledge of God's moral government by reaching the conscience. The apostle Paul states that the human condition is made known by God's law (Rom. 7:9-11). Man is responsible to God for his conduct, held to a standard of conduct and indicted and judged for not upholding that standard, even if he has never read or heard of the Bible (Rom. 2:12-15). According to Paul, man has an innate knowledge of God's attributes (Rom. 1:20), an innate knowledge of God's person (Rom. 1:21), an innate knowledge of God's law

(Rom. 1:32; 2:14-15) and an innate knowledge of God's judgment (Rom. 1:32).

Speak to the conscience

In our apologetic reasoning we must remember that the conscience of man must be reached before cherished intellectual fallacies are abandoned. Arguments against the God of the Bible come from the unbeliever's intellect. The ungodly mind is like a brick wall built to keep God out. It has enmity against him. It refuses to bow to the law of God, 'because the mind set on the flesh is hostile toward God; for it does not subject itself to the law of God, for it is not even able to do so' (Rom. 8:7).

The unbelieving mind weaves arguments and attacks against God. The unregenerate mind is the place of battles against God; it is a place of great hostility against the knowledge of God (Col. 1:21). The mental wall of antagonism against the knowledge of God is hard and immovable and, as a witness of Christ, one should make a habit of skirting it. Learn to speak directly to the conscience. Ray Comfort notes:

The conscience is the only part of human nature that isn't an enemy of God. The conscience is God's ally. It speaks for the law of God. It bears witness (Rom. 2:15). It testifies for God. It is the witness who points out the guilty party in the courtroom. If we want to win our case we must bring out our star witness (God's law) and put it on the stand to give it a voice. We want to stop the mouth of the criminal and that's what the lawful use of the law does (Rom. 3:19; 1 Tim. 1:7-11). It condemns the guilty and drives him to give up his defense, so that he will be forced to look solely to the Judge for mercy.[17]

Preaching the law of God and preaching repentance towards God are necessarily joined to the Holy Spirit's preparation of the sinner. Only the man prepared by God's Spirit goes to war against his own sin and his own sinful nature. The sinner prepared by the Holy Spirit takes God's side against himself. Luther once said,

'Penance remains while self-hate remains.' In other words, no one comes to Christ without being overwhelmed with self-contempt over personal sin. In order to be brought to true repentance, a man must be taken beyond the fear of punishment — to hatred of sin and love of Christ. Repentance begins with sobering thoughts of eternity, then proceeds to conscience-crushing contemplation of personal sin.

The sinner will come willingly if the Spirit of God has prepared him by crushing his conscience over sin and by bringing him to the end of self. Unbelievers stop short of saving faith and repentance when they place their trust in their efforts at personal reformation (what is known as 'legal repentance'). Therefore it is the Spirit's convicting role to bring the sinner to utter bankruptcy of soul and to the point where he is despairing of all self-help. True turning from sin has a palpable desperation about it. The prepared sinner longs for forgiveness and deliverance from sin. The cost of discipleship lived out under the absolute lordship of Christ appeals only to the person who is desperate to be delivered from sin. The prepared person is willing to pay any cost and part with anything in order to have Christ and deliverance.

The man who is genuinely converted never outgrows his amazement at divine forgiveness. His mind and affections are now servants and instruments of God's Word and grace. He continues to glorify God by viewing God's grace from the vantage point of what his sin deserves (Eph. 2:1-16). This is why we preach the law, for it is the beginning of understanding what we justly deserve and it is the beginning of preparing the sinner to appeal to the throne of grace for mercy.

A call for a return to biblical preaching

Conviction of sin

The modern 'gospel' fails to bring the human condition to light; it falls short of producing true conviction of sin. Unless the human condition is exposed in a convincing way that afflicts the conscience, people have little idea of what it is that they are to be saved from. Modern presentations of the gospel tend to emphasize the benefits of salvation rather than the character of God and the sinner's condition. When Christ preached the gospel, he removed all middle ground — he eliminated all grey areas. He emphatically stated that there is no neutral territory between truth and lies, between heaven and hell. Christ's words concerning the gospel made a clear division between men (Luke 11:23).

Christ and the apostles preached the law of God, original sin, the necessity for repentance and the need of a new nature. When the gospel is preached biblically, the soil of the heart will be 'ploughed up' in order to receive the good seed (Matt. 13:1-23). Our self-trust, self-boasting, self-analysis and self-seeking flow from the deception that we can live independently of God. Self-centred man is separated from a holy God by three immense barriers:

- *A bad record* — 'All have sinned....' (Rom. 3:23)
- *A bad heart* — 'For out of the heart come evil thoughts...' (Matt. 15:19)
- *A bad master* — 'Everyone who commits sin is the slave of sin' (John 8:34)

The certainty of God's judgment

God will not let us live as rebels for ever. God's punishment for rebellion is death and judgment. God will call us into account for our actions. The sentence God passes on us is entirely just — it gives us what we have asked for by our rebellion. By our attempts to live independently of God we have said, 'I prefer to live with my back to you; I don't want you telling me what to do. Leave me alone.'[18] 'It is appointed for men to die once, and after this comes judgment' (Heb. 9:27). It is a terrible thing to fall under the sentence of God's judgment. God's judgment on rebels is to withdraw from them, to cut them off from himself permanently. And, since God is the source of all life, light, love, good and blessedness, being cut off from him means death and hell.[19] 'The wages of sin is death...' (Rom. 6:23).

In our alienation from God in this life, we shall experience an accusing conscience which generates fear, guilt and depression. But in the existence to come there will be loss of all friendship and earthly joys for ever (Matt. 8:12; Luke 16:19-31). There will be frightful pains of body and conscience for eternity (Mark 9:48).[20]

Because of his love, God sent his Son into the world

Because of his great love and generosity, God did not leave us to suffer the consequences of our foolish rebellion. He sent his Son, the Lord Jesus, to take our punishment and to bring forgiveness:[21] 'Christ ... died for sins once for all, the just for the unjust, so that He might bring us to God' (1 Peter 3:18). God raised Jesus to life again and appointed him Ruler of the world. Jesus has conquered death. He now gives new life and he will return as Judge. God accepted Jesus' death as payment in full for our sins and raised him from the dead. As God's appointed Ruler over all, Jesus has also been appointed by God to judge the world:[22] 'He will judge the world in righteousness through a Man whom He has appointed' (Acts 17:31; John 5:22-23).

Jesus offers a new life — both now and eternally. Our sins can be forgiven through Christ's death and we can be delivered from rebellion and brought into friendship with God. The pardon that Christ brings to those who trust him assures believers that when he returns he will accept us into his eternal home: '... according to his great mercy [He] has caused us to be born again to a living hope through the resurrection of Jesus Christ from the dead' (1 Peter 1:3). God's gift of new life in Christ removes the barriers which separate us from God (a bad record, a bad heart and a bad master.)

In Christ the believer has:

• *A perfect record* — 'Christ Jesus, who became to us ... righteousness' (1 Cor. 1:30)

- A *new heart* — 'I will give you a new heart' (Ezek. 36:26)
- A *new master* — 'My yoke is easy' (Matt.11:30)

Jesus said of the new life he offers: 'If anyone is thirsty, let him come to Me and drink. He who believes in Me... "From his innermost being will flow rivers of living water"' (John 7:38-39). In this new life, God himself comes to live within us by his Spirit. We experience the joy of a new relationship with God. God's Holy Spirit gives us the 'fruit' of 'love, joy peace, patience, kindness, goodness, faithfulness, gentleness' and 'self-control' (Gal. 5:22). God's Holy Spirit gives us power to overcome feelings of loneliness, stress and fear of people and the future (1 John 4:18). He gives the power to break habits like selfishness, depression, uncontrolled anger, sexual lust, overeating and substance abuse.[23]

We come to Christ by way of repentance and faith. To repent is to turn in sorrow from your sins. Repentance is not our suffering, or the production of good works to earn salvation, but a turning from our sins to the living God through Christ Jesus.

Let the wicked forsake his way,
And the unrighteous man his thoughts;
And let him return to the LORD,
And He will have compassion on him,
And to our God,
For He will abundantly pardon

(Isa. 55:7).

We must trust in Christ Jesus alone: 'Believe in the Lord Jesus, and you will be saved...' (Acts 16:31). Trusting is accepting, receiving and resting on Christ alone as the Saviour from our sins.

Conclusion

A frequently heard cliché concerning the modern church is that it is a mile wide and an inch deep. As with most clichés, there is an element of truth here — actually a large element. The evangelical church has, in some ways, never seemed healthier. Megachurches spring up weekly in many parts of the world. Finances seem to have no limit. Programs of all kinds and for every taste are ubiquitous. Activities are so prolific that church members could literally spend every evening and their whole weekend at the church building. As a matter of fact, all this furious activity reminds me of an old nursery rhyme that goes like this (with liberties taken by me):

> Mary had a little lamb
> Which she loved to keep
> Until it joined the seeker church
> And died for lack of sleep.

As has been documented in this book, the evangelical church is not as healthy as it seems. While there are numerous bright and happy exceptions, the broader picture is troublesome at best. As I travel and engage believers in conversation, I am often amazed at their lack of depth and insight. Spiritual discernment seems to be a lost art — one is almost tempted to say that the church today has none. The very issues addressed in Part I are rampant everywhere.

Whether it is seeker-sensitive dilution of the church and the gospel, emergent liberalism, the deception of the 'prosperity gospel', New Age paganism, or good old-fashioned pragmatism, a short conversation with almost anyone claiming to be a follower of Christ will reveal that he or she has been heavily influenced by one or more of these false approaches to life. The amazing thing is that believers seem totally unaware of this and see no contradiction between these corrupting movements and biblical Christianity.

I spoke recently with a woman who has been a Christian for fifty years and has faithfully attended church over that period. As our conversation turned towards spiritual matters, she immediately sang the praises of several Word of Faith television personalities, most prominently Joel Osteen. She liked what he had to say and how he said it, she told me. 'Yes,' I could not resist saying, 'but what he says is not true; he is not biblical; he is lying to his audience.' This comment did not seem to ruffle her and she quickly agreed with my assessment, yet confirmed that she liked him anyway — along with a whole collection of the worst representatives of true Christianity that I could imagine. She had not been raised on Word of Faith theology, nor did her church preach or practise prosperity teachings, yet she embraced these fallacies. Why? This church had taught her how to live out the first year of her Christian life, but not how to progress further.

The fact is that, while the churches she had been involved in throughout her adult life had not taught Word of Faith ideas, they had not taught much of anything else either. One church had preached the gospel, and by this proclamation the Lord had brought her to himself, but that church has never moved beyond evangelism. Week after week the pastors and evangelists continue to evangelize the evangelized, mixing in perhaps a heavy dose of messages on tithing and church attendance, but little more. Other churches in her background (all in the evangelical tradition) were worse, downplaying the understanding of Scripture, and even the gospel, and replacing it with a social agenda. As a net result, a lifetime of church involvement has left her an immature believer with very little capacity to discern even the most obviously false teaching. And false teaching always leads to false living.

If this anecdote were an isolated case, or limited to a few liberal denominations, there would be little to concern us. But this is increasingly becoming the norm. Children's ministries have for years focused on playtime and colouring; teens have been treated like large children who need to be entertained with contemporary music and a multitude of games and activities; adults are not to be bored with biblical exposition and theology. These practices stem from the late sixties, when the rebellious and spoiled baby-boomers (I can be derogatory because I am in this group!) began to reshape everything (including the church) in their own image. Two generations of Christians have come and are moving through the church, many of whom have never experienced what a biblical church should be. So far removed are many Christians from the New Testament church paradigm that many do not know that anything else exists or ever existed.

It is not unusual for members in good standing in a typical evangelical church to stumble upon a biblical church and be completely surprised by what they have discovered. For years they had realized that something was missing from their Christian life, but not only did they not know what that was, they did not even know what to look for. As one long-time staff member of a seeker-sensitive megachurch said to a friend of mine, 'I know there is more to the Bible than we are getting here; I just don't know what it is.' I believe this is the experience of millions.

As has already been documented, there are many who recognize this spiritual vacuum but are seeking remedies that don't satisfy. Much like the Israelites in Jeremiah's day who were spiritually thirsty, so are we today. But also like those ancient Jews, many are repeating their same sins. God says of his people in Jeremiah 2:13:

> For my people have committed two evils:
> They have forsaken Me,
> The fountain of living waters,

To hew for themselves cisterns,
Broken cisterns
That can hold no water.

Like the Jews, we too are a spiritually thirsty people. And, like the Jews, we tend to ignore the fountain of living water and hew cisterns for ourselves that can never satisfy. If asked, the Old Testament Jews to whom Jeremiah ministered would probably have professed a great interest in spiritual things. They could most likely tick off many ways that they were religious. They would no doubt have claimed at least some allegiance to Jehovah, although they had 'creatively' modified the faith to fit their lifestyles. They would have protested — and indeed they did — against Jeremiah's sermons calling them back to a biblical walk with God. But by Jeremiah's time they had removed themselves so far from the prescribed teachings of their Lord that they could no longer recognize him or his ways, even when these were placed right before their eyes. At the deepest level of their thirst they ignored the 'fountain of life' and set to work digging their own cisterns. Their end was predictable.

Oh, that we would learn from Jeremiah's prophecy! What is needed is thoroughgoing repentance. We have ignored God's ways and God's Word, even as we have paid lip service to the Lord himself. As stated earlier in this book, we need to return to full confidence in the power and the authority of the Word of God, which in turn will cause church leaders to teach once again the full counsel of the Lord. We must expose the unbiblical obstacles that stand in the way and we must boldly claim, 'This is the way of the Lord, walk in it.'

Notes

Preface
1. http://www.barna.org/barna-update/article/19-organic-church/47-americans-embrace-various-alternatives-to-a-conventional-church-experience-as-being-fully-biblical.

Introduction
1. As quoted by Jim Thomas, *Answering the Big Questions About God,* (Eugene, Oregon: Harvest House Publishers 2000/2001), p.21.
2. www.barna.org/FlexPage.aspx?Page=BarnaUpdateNarrow&BarnaUpdate ID=216&P.
3. *Ibid.*
4. www.barna.org/FlexPage.aspx?Page=BarnaUpdateNarrow&BarnaUpdate ID =154.
5. www.barna.org/FlexPage.aspx?Page=CMD=Print.
6. *Ibid.*
7. *Ibid.*

Chapter 1 — The Seeker-Sensitive Adjustment
1. It is not my purpose to explore in detail at this time the Willow Creek church model. I have written extensively on the seeker-sensitive church movement in my book, *This Little Church Went to Market* (Darlington: Evangelical Press, 2005). Please consult that book for more information regarding the methods and teachings of those who embrace this paradigm.
2. A generation reaching adulthood in the 1980s and 1990s and perceived to be disaffected, directionless, or irresponsible and reluctant to participate in society.
3. www.christianitytoday.com/ct/2006/october/5.25.html.
4. All quotes by Greg Hawkins are from Hawkins' video clip found at www.revealnow.com/story.asp?storyid=48.
5. Unless otherwise stated, all quotes by Bill Hybels are taken from his video clip at the 2007 Leadership Summit found at www.http://revealnow.com /story.asp?storyid=31.

6. www.willowcreek.com/AboutUs.html.
7. www.willowcreek.com/shift2008/AboutShift.html.
8. *Ibid.*
9. www.willowcreek.com/AboutUs.html.

Chapter 2 — The Emergent Church Goes Ancient

1. *Christianity Today*, January 2009, p.13.
2. *Ibid.*, p.14.
3. Mark Galli, 'Ancient-Future People,' *Christianity Today*, February 2008, p.7.
4. Chris Armstrong, 'The Future Lies in the Past,' *Christianity Today*, February 2008, p.24.
5. *Ibid.*, p.25.
6. Robert E. Webber, *Ancient-Future Faith* (Grand Rapids: Baker Book House, 1999), p.7.
7. *Ibid.*, p.17.
8. *Ibid.*, p.13.
9. *Ibid.*, p.16.
10. Armstrong, 'The Future Lies in the Past,' p.26.
11. *Ibid.*
12. *Ibid.*
13. As quoted by Armstrong, 'The Future Lies in the Past,' p.28.
14. Armstrong, 'The Future Lies in the Past,'p.28.
15. *Ibid.*, p.29.
16. *Ibid.*, pp.23, 29.
17. www.usnews.com/articles/news/national/2007/12/13/a-return-to-tradition_print.htm.
18. Jennifer Trafton, 'Rediscovering Benedict,' *Christian History and Biography*, issue 93, p.6.
19. Jennifer Hevelone-Harper, 'Radical Christians', *Christian History and Biography*, issue 93, p.7.
20. Findings summarized from http://www.christianpost.com/article/20080227/31344_2_Mars_Hill_Pastor_Ditches_%27Emerging%27_Label _ for_Jesus.htm.
21. http://en.wikipedia.org/wiki/Lectio_Divina
22. James L. Wakefield, *Sacred Listening* (Grand Rapids: Baker, 2006), p.23. This quote is taken from Peterson's book, *Eat This Book* (Grand Rapids, Eerdmans, 2006), p.116, with the italics in the original.
23. Mark Yaconelli, *Contemplative Youth Ministry* (Grand Rapids: Zondervan, 2006), p.85.

24. Kenneth Boa, *The Trinity, a Journal* (Colorado Springs: NavPress, 2001), p.13.

25. *Ibid.*, pp.14, 15.

26. *Ibid.*, pp.16, 17.

27. *Ibid.*, p.19.

28. *Ibid.*, p.20.

29. Yaconelli, *Contemplative Youth Ministry*, p.86.

30. Robert Benson, *In Constant Prayer* (Nashville, Tennessee: Thomas Nelson, 2008) pp.4, 19-28, 114, 116 (Note, my edition of *In Constant Prayer* is a prepublication edition and page numbers may be different in the final published format).

31. Chris Armstrong, 'Re-Monking the Church,' *Christian History & Biography*, issue 93, Winter 2007, p.34.

32. *Ibid.*, p.35.

33. As quoted in Wakefield, *Sacred Listening*, p.1.

34. *Ibid.*, pp.1-2.

35. http://www.nwjesuits.org/JesuitSpirituality/SpiritualExercises.html

36. Wakefield, *Sacred Listening*, p.17.

37. *Ibid.*, p.18.

38. James K. A. Smith, *Who's Afraid of Postmodernism?* (Grand Rapids: Baker Academic, 2006), p.140.

39. While these practices are commonly recommended in emergent and A-F literature today, for documentation see Mike King, *Presence-Centered Youth Ministry* (Downers Grove, Illinois: IVP Books, 2006), pp.87-96, 121-34, 170.

40. Brian McLaren, *Finding Our Way Again* (Nashville, Tennessee: Thomas Nelson, p.2008), pp.150-51. (It should be noted that the edition of *Finding Our Way Again* cited in this chapter was a prepublication edition and page numbers may be subject to change in the final published edition.)

41. *Ibid.*, p.160.

42. *Ibid.*, p.162.

43. *Ibid.*, p.18.

44. *Ibid.*, p.19.

45. Webber, *Ancient-Future Faith*, p.19.

46. *Ibid.*, p.24.

47. *Ibid.*, p.95.

48. *Ibid.*, p.176.

49. *Ibid.*, p.184.

50. Tony Lane, *A Concise History of Christian Thought* (Grand Rapids: Baker Academic, 2006), pp.62-3.

51. Webber, *Ancient-Future Faith*, p.194.

52. Lane, *A Concise History of Christian Thought,* p.63.
53. *Ibid.,* p.62.
54. *Ibid.,* p.41.
55. Webber, *Ancient-Future Faith,* p.200.
56. *Ibid.,* p.193.
57. Andy Crouch, 'The Emergent Mystique,' *Christianity Today,* November 2004, p.38.
58. Webber, *Ancient-Future Faith,* p.146.
59. *Ibid.,* pp.147-9.
60. *Ibid.,* p.189.
61. *Ibid.,* p.177.
62. *Ibid.*
63. *Ibid.,* p.201.
64. *Ibid.,* p.135.
65. McLaren, *Finding Our Way Again,* pp.179-80.
66. St John of the Cross, *Dark Night of the Soul,* translated and edited by E. Allison Peers (New York: Image Books, 1990), p.87.
67. *Ibid.,* p.123.
68. Teresa of Avila, *Interior Castle,* translated by E. Allison Peers (New York: Image Books, 1989), p.88.
69. *Ibid.,* p.173.
70. Armstrong, 'The Future Lies in the Past,' p.29.

Chapter 3 — Invasion of paganism
1. Eckhart Tolle, *A New Earth, Awakening to Your Life's Purpose* (New York: Penguin Group, 2006), pp.5-6.
2. *Ibid.,* p.259.
3. *Ibid.,* pp.4, 26, 106.
4. *Ibid.,* p.28.
5. *Ibid.,* pp.57, 60, 64, 79, 128.
6. *Ibid.,* p.71.
7. *Ibid.,* p.220.
8. William Young, *The Shack* (Los Angeles: Windblown, 2007), pp.194, 204.
9. *Ibid.,* p. 110.
10. The concept that God is 'in' everything is known as 'panentheism' — an Eastern belief akin to pantheism, which teaches that God *is* everything. In reality there is very little difference between the two.
11. Young, *The Shack,* p.198.
12. *Ibid.,* p. 233.

13. *Ibid.,* p. 227.
14. *Ibid.,* p.112.
15. Unless otherwise stated, all quotations are taken from *The Secret* DVD.
16. Yusufu Turaki, *Foundations of African Traditional Religion and Worldview* (Nairobi, Kenya: WordAlive Publishers Limited, 2006), pp.15, 107, 117.
17. *Ibid.,* pp.19, 33.
18. *Ibid.,* pp.23-9.
19. *Ibid.,* p.24.
20. *Ibid.,* pp.68-70, 81-7.
21. *Ibid.,* pp.35-6, 47-8, 56-7, 89-96.
22. *Ibid.,* p.96.
23. *Ibid.,* p.78.
24. *Ibid.,* pp.97-8.
25. *Ibid.,* pp.99-104.
26. *Areopagus Journal,* July-August 2006, p.24.
27. *Ibid.,* p.23.
28. Ron Rhodes, *The Challenge of the Cults and New Religions* (Grand Rapids: Zondervan, 2001), pp.104-5.
29. *Ibid.,* p.105.
30. *Ibid.,* p.106.
31. *Ibid.,* p.107.
32. Rhonda Byrne, *The Secret* (New York, NY: Atria Books, 2006), p.164.
33. *Ibid.,* p.83.
34. W. K. Clifford, 'The Ethics of Belief', found at www.skeptic.com/eskeptic/07-03-07.html.

Chapter 4 — The Prosperity Gospel Goes Mainstream
1. http://www.usnews.com/articles/news/national/2008/02/15/behind-the-prosperity-gospel.html.
2. Hank Hanegraaff, *Christianity in Crisis* (Eugene, Oregon: Harvest House Publishers, 1993), pp.74, 75.
3. *Ibid.,* p.80.
4. *Ibid.,* pp.83, 84.
5. Michael Horton, *Christless Christianity* (Grand Rapids: Baker, 2008), p.68.
6. http://churchrevelance.com/top/100-largest-churches-in-america-of-2008. It is worthy of note that, according to this source, attendance has dropped by 3,500 people from the previous year — a virtual megachurch in its own right.
7. Joel Osteen, *Your Best Life Now* (New York: Faith Word, 2004), p.212.
8. *Ibid.,* p.5.

9. *Ibid.*, pp.126-7.
10. *Ibid.*, p.35.
11. *Ibid.*, p.78.
12. *Ibid.*, p.114.
13. *Ibid.*, p.5.
14. *Ibid.*, p.25.
15. *Ibid.*, p.35.
16. *Ibid.*, pp.196-8.
17. *Ibid.*, p.82.
18. *Ibid.*, p.40.
19. *Ibid.*, p.41.
20. *Ibid.*, pp.41-2.
21. *Ibid.*, p.43.
22. *Ibid.*, p.8.
23. *Ibid.*, p.33.
24. *Ibid.*, pp.57-8.
25. *Ibid.*, p.67.
26. See Osteen, *Your Best Life Now,* pp.10, 14, 18, 30-31, 33, 61, 76, 79-83, 87-9, 104, 115, 129-30, 134, 164.
27. *Ibid.*, p.viii.
28. See, for example, Osteen, *Your Best Life Now,* pp.12, 23, 73, 122, 161, 167, 201-2, 229, 280-81, 292.
29. *Ibid.*, pp.4, 7-8, 27, 111-12, 125, 127, 199-200, 246.
30. *Ibid.*, p.199.
31. *Ibid.*, pp.151, 176.
32. *Ibid.*, pp.181-2.
33. *Ibid.*, pp.207-9.
34. *Ibid.*, p.247.
35. *Ibid.*, p.248.
36. *Ibid.*, p.205.
37. *Ibid.*, p.4.
38. *Ibid.*, pp.5-6.
39. *Ibid.*, p.101.
40. *Ibid.*, p.104.
41. *Ibid.*, p.33.
42. *Ibid.*, p.72.
43. *Ibid.*, p.74.
44. *Ibid.*, p.306.
45. *Ibid.*, p.13.
46. *Ibid.*, p.109.

47. *Ibid.*, p.122.
48. *Ibid.*, p.123.
49. *Ibid.*, p.124.
50. *Ibid.*, p.125.
51. *Ibid.*, p.129.
52. *Ibid.*, p.130.
53. *Ibid.*, p.132.

Chapter 5 — The Challenge of Pragmatism

1. Donald Miller, *Blue Like Jazz* (Nashville: Thomas Nelson, 2003), p.42.
2. *Ibid.*, p.23.
3. *Ibid.*, pp.207-8.
4. Brian Morley, 'Understanding Our Postmodern World,' *Think Biblically*, gen. ed. John MacArthur (Wheaton: Crossway, 2003), p.140.
5. Gordon H. Clark, *A Christian Philosophy of Education* (Jefferson Md.: Trinity Foundation, 1988), p.158.
6. As quoted in George M. Marsden, *Fundamentalism and American Culture* (Oxford: Oxford University Press, 1982), p.137.
7. Webber, *Ancient-Future Faith,* p.19.
8. David Bebbington, *The Dominance of Evangelicalism* (Downers Grove: InterVarsity Press, 2005), p.148.
9. *Ibid.*, p.164.
10. *Ibid.*
11. Iain H. Murray, *Evangelicalism Divided* (Edinburgh: Banner of Truth, 2000), p.5.
12. Joel R. Beeke and Ray B. Lanning, 'The Transforming Power of Scripture,' *Sola Scriptura!,* gen ed. Don Kistler (Morgan, PA: Soli Deo Gloria Publications, 1995), p.253.
13. Brian McLaren, *A Generous Orthodoxy* (El Cajon, Ca: Youth Specialties Books, 2004), p.223.
14. Rob Bell, *Velvet Elvis* (Grand Rapids: Zondervan, 2005), p.21.
15. *Ibid.*, p.26.
16. *Ibid.*
17. *Ibid.*
18. http://www.seedsofcompassion.org/involved/interreligious_day.asp.
19. *Ibid.*
20. Murray, *Evangelicalism Divided,* p.12.
21. *Ibid.*
22. Murray, *Evangelicalism Divided,* p.11.

23. See Marsden, *Fundamentalism and American Culture,* pp.171-228. (This was especially true of the old-line Presbyterians represented by Princeton Theological Seminary, Dispensationalists and the Holiness movement).

24. Murray, *Evangelicalism Divided,* p.14.

25. Jim Henderson and Matt Casper, *Jim and Casper Go to Church* (Tyndale House Publishers, 2007, p.xxxv (pre-publication document).

26. John Piper, *The Supremacy of God in Preaching* (Grand Rapids: Baker Books, 1999), pp.10-11.

27. George Gallup, Jr., *The Next American Spirituality, Finding God in the Twenty-First Century* (Colorado Springs: Cook, 2000), p.129.

28. *Ibid.,* p.130.

Chapter 6 — The New Atheism

1. R. Albert Mohler Jr., *Atheism Remix, a Christian Confronts the New Atheists* (Wheaton: Crossway, 2008), p.19.

2. *Ibid.,* p.39.

3. Richard Dawkins, *The God Delusion* (Boston: Houghton Mifflin, 2006), p.5.

4. www.foxnews.com/story/0,2933,450445,00.html

5. *Ibid.*

6. *Ibid.*

7. Dawkins, *The God Delusion,* p.31.

8. *Ibid.,* p.251.

9. *Ibid.,* p.51.

10. *Ibid.,* pp.77-9.

11. *Ibid.,* pp.157-8.

12. *Ibid.,* p.92.

13. *Ibid.,* p.100.

14. *Ibid.,* p.158.

15. *Ibid.,* p.113.

16. *Ibid.,* p.116.

17. *Ibid.,* p.121.

18. *Ibid.,* p.136.

19. *Ibid.,* p.140.

20. *Ibid.,* p.141.

21. *Ibid.,* p.143.

22. www.foxnews.com/story/0,2933,450445,00.html

23. Dawkins, *The God Delusion,* p.226.

24. *Ibid.,* p.216.

25. *Ibid.*

26. www.thedenverchannel.com/news/17977308/detail.html
27. Richard Dawkins, *A Devil's Chaplain* (London: Weidenfeld and Nicolson, p. 2003), p.81.
28. Alister McGrath and Joanna Collicutt McGrath, *The Dawkins Delusion* (Downers Grove: InterVarsity Press, 2007), pp.96-7.
29. Terry Eagleton, 'Lunging, Flailing, Mispunching': A Review of Richard Dawkins' *The God Delusion,' London Review of Books*, vol. 28, no. 20, 19 October 2006.
30. Mohler, *Atheism Remix,* p.79.
31. Dawkins, *The God Delusion,* p.100.
32. Timothy Keller, *The Reason for God* (New York: Dutton, 2008), p.89.
33. http://www.calvin.edu/academic/philosophy/virtual_library/articles/plantinga_alvin/two_dozen_or_so_theistic_arguments.pdf.
34. William Lane Craig, 'God is Not Dead Yet,' *Christianity Today*, July 2008, pp.22-7.
35. *Ibid.,* p.26.
36. Jean-Paul Sartre, *Nausea* (New York: New Directions Publishing, 1964), p.133.
37. Dawkins, *The God Delusion,* p.100.
38. *Ibid.,* p.163.
39. *Ibid.,* p.199.
40. *Ibid.,* p.216.
41. As quoted in Keller, *The Reason for God,* p.36.
42. McGrath, *The Dawkins Delusion,* p.96.

Chapter 7 — A Renewed Confidence in the Word of God

1. Brian D. McLaren and Tony Campolo, *Adventures in Missing the Point* (Grand Rapids: Zondervan, 2003), p.84.
2. For more on postmodernism see my book *This Little Church Stayed Home* (Darlington: Evangelical Press, 2006), pp.21-54.
3. Os Guinness, *Time for Truth* (Grand Rapids: Baker Books, 2000), p.52.
4. Donald Bloesch, *Essentials of Evangelical Theology* (Peabody, MA: Prince Press, 2001), p.275.
5. *Ibid.,* p.268.
6. McLaren and Campolo, *Adventures in Missing the Point,* p.78.
7. *Ibid.,* p.77.
8. *Ibid.,* p.79.
9. *Ibid.,* p.89.
10. Personal letter from Dr James Blankenship.
11. Michael J. Vlach, 'Crisis in America's Churches: Bible Knowledge at All-Time Low', www.theologicalstudies.citymax.com/page/page/1573625.

12. As quoted in 'Church and Community or Community and Church?', Gary L. W. Johnson & Ronald N. Gleason, *Reforming or Conforming?* (Wheaton: Crossway, 2008), p.174.

13. *Ibid.*

14. As quoted in Murray, *Evangelicalism Divided*, p.254.

15. Francis Schaeffer, *The Complete Works of Francis Schaeffer, The God Who Is There* (Wheaton: Crossway, 1982), p.47.

16. Vlach, 'Crisis in America's Churches'.

Chapter 8 — Pastoring with Both Eyes Open

1. Steve Brown, 'Developing a Christian Mean Streak,' *Leadership* (vol. VIII, no. 2), Spring 1987, pp.32-7.

Chapter 10 — The Power of a Christian Worldview in Evangelism

1. Francis Schaeffer, Address at the University of Notre Dame, April 1981, quoted in Nancy Pearcey, *Total Truth* (Wheaton: Crossway Books, 2004), p.15.

2. Cornelius Van Til, *The Defense of the Faith* (Phillipsburg: Presbyterian and Reformed Publishing, 1955), pp.173, 196.

3. David Wells, *God in the Wasteland* (Grand Rapids: William B. Eerdmans, 1994), pp.100, 101.

4. D. A. Carson, 'The Supremacy of Christ in Postmodern Culture' (*Desiring God,* Conference, 2006).

5. Christopher Gornold-Smith, 'Apologetics in a Postmodern World' (the 'Help Center,' Chi Alpha Campus Ministries, USA, 2003), p.5.

6. Del Tackett, 'What's a Worldview Anyway?' *Focus on the Family* (July/August, 2004), p.9.

7. Philip Edgecumbe Hughes, 'Crucial Biblical Passages for Christian Apologetics,' *Jerusalem and Athens,* E. R. Geehan, ed. (Phillipsburg: Presbyterian and Reformed Publishing, 1971), p.136.

8. Peter Jones, 'Framing the Issues; Finding our Voice for the Twenty-first Century', *The Christian Response to Neo-paganism* (Escondido: Christian Witness to a Pagan Planet, 2007).

9. Kim Riddlebarger, 'Francis Schaeffer: Taking the Roof Off' (The Apologetics of Francis Schaeffer, www.monergism.com).

10. James F. Stitzinger, 'Apologetics and Evangelism Th 701' (Sun Valley: The Master's Seminary, 1999), pp.18-19, 24-6, 36.

11. John Frame, *Apologetics to the Glory of God* (Phillipsburg: Presbyterian and Reformed Publishing, 1994), pp.120, 121.

12. Tim Keller, 'The Supremacy of Christ in Postmodern Culture' (*Desiring God,* Conference, 2006).
13. Carson, 'The Supremacy of Christ in Postmodern Culture.'
14. *Ibid.*
15. Van Til, *The Defense of the Faith,* p.29.
16. John Whitcomb, 'Contemporary Apologetics,' published articles on contemporary apologetics in *Bibliotheca Sacra,* April 1977, which became recorded lectures available through the ministry of John C. Whitcomb.
17. Stitzinger, 'Apologetics and Evangelism Th 701,' pp.116-17, 219.
18. Carson, 'The Supremacy of Christ in Postmodern Culture.'

Chapter 11 — Sharing the Gospel in a Culture of Truth-Suppressors
1. Riddlebarger, 'Francis Schaeffer: Taking the Roof Off.'
2. *Ibid.*
3. Pearcey, *Total Truth,* p.25.
4. Riddlebarger, 'Francis Schaeffer: Taking the Roof Off.'
5. *Ibid.*
6. Stitzinger, 'Apologetics and Evangelism', pp.58, 99, 101, 113.
7. William Edgar, 'Two Christian Warriors: Cornelius Van Til and Francis A. Schaeffer Compared', *Westminister Theological Journal,* vol. 57, no.1 (Spring 1995), p.65.
8. Tackett, 'What's a Worldview Anyway?', p.8.
9. Greg L. Bahnsen, *Van Til's Apologetic, Readings & Analysis* (Phillips-burg: P&R Publishing, 1998), p.439.
10. *Ibid.,* p.97.
11. John M. Frame, 'Van Til on Antithesis', *Westminster Theological Journal,* vol. 57, no. 1 (Spring 1995), p.101.
12. Bahnsen, *Van Til's Apologetic,* p.424.
13. Van Til, *The Defense of the Faith,* p.67.
14. *Ibid.,* p.417.
15. Stitzinger, *Apologetics and Evangelism,* pp.118, 126.
16. *Ibid.,* pp.122, 126, 127.
17. Greg Bahnsen, *Always Ready* (Atlanta, GA: American Vision, 1996), p.83.
18. Bahnsen, *Van Til's Apologetic,* p.448.
19. Stitzinger, *Apologetics and Evangelism,* p.97.
20. Richard B. Gaffin Jr., 'Some Epistemological Reflections on 1 Corinthians 2:6-16', *Westminster Theological Journal,* vol. 57, no. 1 (Spring 1995), pp.106-10.

Chapter 12 — Recovering the Neglected Elements of the Biblical Gospel

1. Greg Bahnsen, 'At War with the Word: The Necessity of Biblical Antithesis', www.reformed.org (2001), p.1.
2. Ibid., p.16.
3. Ibid., p.18.
4. Greg Bahnsen, Always Ready (Atlanta, GA: American Vision, 1996), pp.157-9.
5. Michael Kruger, 'The Sufficiency of Scripture in Apologetics', The Master's Seminary Journal, vol. 12, no. 1 (Spring 2001), p.72.
6. Thom Notaro, Van Til and Evidences (Phillipsburg, NJ: Presbyterian and Reformed Publishing, 1980), p.40.
7. Frame, Apologetics to the Glory of God, p.232.
8. Edward Morgan, The Life and Times of Howell Harris (Denton, TX: The Need of the Times, 1998), p.71.
9. Ibid., p.74.
10. Thomas Wilcox, Christ is All (London: J. W. Pasham, 1782, reprinted by Chapel Library, Pensacola, FL, 1999 under the title God's Gift to Sinners), pp.24-5.
11. Ibid., pp.257-8.
12. J. C. Philpot, The Heavenly Birth and its Earthly Counterfeit (Chapel Library reprint), p.4.
13. Joseph Lo Sardo, 'Errors in Modern Evangelism', www.sermonaudio. com (5/7/06).
14. Robert Bolton, Afflicted Consciences (London, 1631), p.175.
15. Ernest F. Kevan, The Grace of Law (Morgan, PA: Soli Deo Gloria Publications, 1993 reprint), p.265.
16. Douglas W. Phillips, Esq., 'Do Laws and Standards Evolve?' Impact no. 303 (Institute for Creation Research, 1998).
17. Ray Comfort, 'Conversions True and False', audio message, www. livingwaters.com.
18. Two Ways to Live, www.mathiasmedia.com.au/2wtl/
19. Ibid.
20. C. John Miller, Powerful Evangelism for the Powerless (Phillipsburg, NJ: Presbyterian and Reformed, 1980), p.149.
21. Two Ways to Live.
22. Ibid.
23. Miller, Powerful Evangelism for the Powerless, pp.147-8.

The only issue I have with Gary Gilley is that I now need to buy another highlighter! With the skill of a surgeon and the passion of a pastor he draws irresistible attention to major flaws in modern evangelicalism and points unerringly to the remedies that are urgently needed. Everyone in church leadership should read this book — and then encourage their followers to do the same!

Dr John Blanchard

Christian author, international conference speaker and evangelist

When people ask me for the best, most trustworthy resources analysing the current evangelical drift, I always start by recommending two books by Gary Gilley: *This Little Church Went to Market* and *This Little Church Stayed Home*. Gilley's brilliant new book, *This Little Church Had None,* makes the series a must-have trilogy. This is an excellent, hard-hitting critique of the pragmatic, poll-driven styles that dominate evangelical ministries today, punctuated with a serious, sobering call for a return to biblical principles.

Phil Johnson

Executive Director, Grace to You

Here the reader finds essential insights into the various anti- or sub-Christian movements outside and inside the church that oppose true gospel preaching today. Paganism, Gnosticism, the 'New Atheism', Pragmatism and the leftward-leaning Emergent Church are carefully and accurately analysed and various crucial antidotes are helpfully given. These include the importance of an orthodox doctrine of Scripture and of the person of the sovereign God, a courageous exercise of leadership based on Scripture, and a winsome and creative worldview evangelism, unapologetically announcing the antithesis between the Truth and the Lie. In a time when this little church we know as evangelicalism has none, or few, of its once-defining elements, this book brings an important and timely reminder of the need for the church to return to the biblical basics that were once and for all delivered to the saints.

Peter Jones, Ph.D,
Director, *truthXchange,* Scholar-in-Residence and Adjunct
Professor, Westminster Seminary California

Relating to the state of the American church today, I commend Gary Gilley's clear thinking, cogent commentary and compelling conclusions in *This Little Church Had None* as a sequel to *This Little Church Went to Market* and *This Little Church Stayed Home.* His third volume is a must-read for pastors and laypeople alike.

Richard Mayhue, Th.D.
Senior VP and Dean, The Master's Seminary

Gary's previous two books in this series have demonstrated his unique ability to use his clear understanding of God's Word to analyse and explain teaching and practices which are often confused and destructive to the church. This is done with a clarity and simplicity that is often lacking in such analysis. *This Little Church Had None* continues this tradition, focusing even greater attention on the place of God's truth in the ministry of the church. What Gary presents in this book is foundational to everything God intends his church to be and to do. As a pastor, I am greatly encouraged to have such a resource available for myself and my people.

Gil Rugh
Senior Pastor, Indian Hills Community Church, Lincoln, Nebraska

The book *This Little Church Had None* should be read by every pastor, church leader, youth pastor, Sunday School teacher, professor of future church leaders, and Christians in general. Dr Gary E. Gilley, veteran pastor of Southern View Chapel, Springfield,